# The Internet Fact Finder for Lawyers

## How to Find Anything on the Net

by Joshua D. Blackman
with David Jank

ABA American Bar Association
Law Practice Management Section

Cover design by Lisa Scalise.


Printed in the United States of America.

Library of Congress Catalog Card Number 98-70386
ISBN 1-57073-535-2

02 01 00 99 98 5 4 3 2 1

# Contents



## Part One: How to Conduct Research on the Net

## *Part Three: Putting It into Practice*

# About the Authors

**Josh Blackman** founded the Legal Research Group at FIND/SVP in New York City, which provides research and consulting services to some 2,500 business and legal clients. A lawyer, Mr. Blackman's background includes some ten years in the computer industry as a mainframe programmer and technical writer. He has used the Internet to conduct research for more than five years, and has offered Internet training in live training sessions, as well as online. Mr. Blackman speaks frequently to Bar association groups, and has appeared several times on various national forums, including CNN*fn*, regarding the online industry. He edits *The Internet Lawyer* newsletter, is the "Legal Internet" columnist for *Law Office Computing* magazine, and is author of five books, including *How to Use the Internet for Legal Research,* published by FIND/SVP.

**David Jank** has over twenty years experience in the areas of information services design and consulting. Mr. Jank has worked in a variety of capacities for systems developers and integrators, and specializes in library automation and information delivery. Currently, he is serving as an adjunct consultant for the People to People Citizens Ambassador Program, with which he travels and speaks on trends in information technology. David holds a Master of Science degree from Simmons College, and a Bachelor's degree from Northeastern University. He served two years as national chair of the Special Libraries Association Telecommunications Division, for which he received the professional achievement award. He is a featured author for the 1997 "What Else You Can Do With a Library Degree," has spoken at a variety of trade shows and conferences, and has been a contributing writer for a number of library and information technology publications.

# Acknowledgments

THIS BOOK WAS MADE MORE INTERESTING because of the generous contributions of the following individuals, who shared their time and experiences so that you can understand how to use the Net to find anything. You'll find their comments scattered throughout the text: Harold J. Bursztajn, Ted Claypoole, Bruce Dorner, Jonathan Ezor, Kevin Grierson, Doug Humes, Robert J. O'Brien, Cathy Pennington Paunov, Wes Pittman, Greg L. Siskind, Cleveland Thornton, Ben Wright, and Michael C. Zusman.

David Jank contributed a good deal of the ideas and writing found in the "How to Conduct Research on the Net" and "The Internet Library" portions of this book. As a Senior Consultant and my colleague at the research firm FIND/SVP, as a seasoned librarian, and as someone steeped in how to be a smart researcher, David's insights and skills helped make this a better book.

The good folks at the American Bar Association have propelled an idea into the finished product you're reading now. Thanks to Beverly Loder, Jeff Flax, Tim Johnson, and Burgess Allison for everything. And special thanks to the Sage of Park Slope, who helps make everything good and true.

To my brothers, Adam and Jonathan,
who continually remind me
that life is like a shark:
If it doesn't move forward,
you end up with a dead shark.

# Foreword

SO YOU'RE CONVINCED that the Internet, that living embodiment of McLuhan's global village, contains resources to improve your productivity, keep abreast of breaking trends in the practice of law, and enable you to better serve your clients. You are eager to make the most of your new software for accessing and browsing the World Wide Web. You know that the fact you need to confound opposing counsel and win that summary judgment motion is out there somewhere. But every time you log on and start surfing, you get mired in the vast morass of fascinating information and never seem to find what you need.

The ABA Section of Law Practice Management has always assisted lawyers to integrate new technologies into their practices. To this end, we have published a line of books on using the Internet, including *The Lawyer's Guide to the Internet, The Lawyer's Quick Guide to Netscape® Navigator,* and *The Lawyer's Quick Guide to Microsoft® Internet Explorer,* all by G. Burgess Allison; *The Lawyer's Guide to Creating Web Pages* by Kenneth Johnson; and *The Lawyer's Guide to Marketing on the Internet* by Gregory Siskind and Timothy Moses. We've listened to your requests for a similar practical tool for lawyers who want to use the Internet to do general research. *The Internet Fact Finder for Lawyers: How to Find Anything on the Net,* by Josh Blackman with David Jank, is our answer.

Mr. Blackman draws on his expertise as the editor of *The Internet Lawyer,* a highly respected source of law-related Internet information. With Mr. Jank's assistance, Mr. Blackman walks you through a wealth of Internet resource sites; teaches you how to think like a researcher (and avoid wandering down those blind alleys that look so inviting); educates you in what is worth paying for and what you can get for free; helps you evaluate newsgroup information; points you to expert witness and competitive intelligence resources; leads you to primary, secondary, and tertiary sources; assists you with finding an Internet service provider; discusses

Web browsers and search engines; reveals sources of medical information; and much more. Along the way, you will be informed and entertained by the true stories of lawyers who have not only "been there and done that," but are willing to share with you what they have learned.

Most of our readers are familiar with and can perform basic online legal research (for those who need help, we offer *Computer-Assisted Legal Research,* by Susan Cochard and Samantha Whitney-Ulane). But proficiency in finding online nonlegal information is equally important and less easy to obtain. To fill this need, LPM Publishing is pleased to provide this reference work, which also manages to be a very good read. We trust that it will increase your efficiency at and enjoyment of Internet research.

Robert J. Conroy
Judith L. Grubner
Co-Chairs, LPM Publishing

# Preface

IN THE INTEREST OF BEING UNDERSTOOD by novices and experts alike, every effort has been made to keep the language and concepts in these pages as clear and simple as possible. It is possible, however, that a few of the terms used here may be new to you. In that case, consider clicking over to the Beginner's Web Glossary (http://www.cwru.edu/help/webglossary.html) offered online by Case Western University.

The prior sentence expresses some of the assumptions made in the course of writing this book. For example, I've assumed you are already somewhat familiar with the World Wide Web, and with Web browsers like Netscape Navigator or Microsoft Explorer. In addition, I've assumed you recognize the string of characters in parentheses that will take you to the Web Glossary. For those not familiar with such things, the string is known as a Uniform Resource Locator or URL. The URL is the standard way of expressing the location of data on the Web, and is used throughout this book. For more information, take a look at the Beginner's Guide to URLs (http://www.ncsa.uiuc.edu/demoweb/url-primer.html).

The other important thing for you to know about this book is that almost without exception, the resources discussed here are free of any incremental charge. That means that all you need to access the services and databases discussed is a computer with Web access. You won't incur any fees by accessing the URLs listed. This is an important distinction to be made at this time in the Web's evolution. Most database providers and publishers, including LEXIS/NEXIS, for example, are providing Internet access to their traditional fee-based services. If you access the LEXIS database via the Net, you will incur charges just as you will if you access LEXIS via the more traditional software provided by LEXIS.

Finally, there's an online component to this book, which provides updates to some of the URL lists included here. For example, there's a "Basic Library Resources" collection, etc. You can find these update pages at the Internet Lawyer site (http://www.internetlawyer.com/facts).

# INTRODUCTION

## *How Legal Professionals Can Use the Net for General Research Purposes*

IN LEGAL PRACTICE, research involves much more than the case law, statutes, and regulations explained in law school. For example, medical malpractice lawyers need to know how to find out about anatomy and about locating medical experts. Product liability lawyers need to know how to find out about corporate parent-subsidiary relationships and about products sold by various companies. The Internet is extremely well suited to such fact-finding.

While WESTLAW and other traditional legal research tools provide access to the law, they do not assist in the collection of factual information. The best researchers know that there are many ways to access information. The key to successful, efficient research is knowing where to start. As the Internet continues to widen in breadth, it is increasingly becoming a first stop for research of all sorts, including traditional legal research and, in particular, factual research. The openness of the Net, which enables virtually anyone to publish on it, has resulted in a continually expanding collection that covers the scope of human knowledge. This is not to say that you can find everything on the Net, but it is likely you will find something related to your research, something that will point you in a productive direction, if not actually answer your precise question.

Lawyers have an obligation to clients (and to themselves, to remain competitive) to have access to the most comprehensive, cost-effective research resources. The Internet provides an unparalleled tool to find the facts relevant to legal issues.

In fact, lawyers may run the risk of competency claims if they do not have access to the Net. At least one federal court has held that to avoid negligence and to satisfy due diligence considerations, lawyers must be plugged in. Seventh Circuit Judge Kanne wrote that in the context of a Rule l0b-5 securities fraud action, "a reasonable investor is presumed to have information available in the public domain," and that the "information superhighway" is a source for such information (*Whirlpool Financial Corporation v. GN Holdings, Inc.,* 1995 U.S. App. LEXIS 27600, http://www.law.emory.edu/7circuit/sept95/95-1292.html).

If you are not yet convinced that you should bother with the Internet, or if you are uncertain whether anything of practical value is available on the Net, here are a few practicing lawyers describing how they have used the Net to solve problems.

## ■ SUCCESS STORY: WES PITTMAN

Wes Pittman, Esq., of Pittman, Manuel, Thompson & Perry in Panama City, Florida, describes how he finished a trial for which he had used the Net to generate some ideas for opening statements and summations. He says that it worked "marvelously well:"

> I represented a plaintiff in a personal injury case. The defendant was a drunk driver who crossed the center line of a highway one dark, rainy night and struck her car head-on. I had a claim not only for compensatory but also for punitive damages. Under Florida law, we are permitted to argue that punitives are to deter flagrant conduct by the defendant and by others, and we are able to argue that the conduct is pervasive, et cetera, much like in other jurisdictions. I needed to use only one search phrase, *drunk driving,* to generate more than forty-nine thousand hits and to find, within the first twenty-five, two great ideas to use. Both ideas related to the widespread practice of drinking while driving and how it has become a joking matter. I took it one step further, of course, to say in closing that the only way to keep people like the defendant from continuing to make drunk driving a joke is to send a message by a punitive award.
>
> The two hits that were so useful were about a card game called Drunk Driver, Drunk Driver, in which successive cards are dealt, each accompanied by the consumption of an entire drink, until the driver "safely makes it off the road" (all the cards are dealt). [The second useful site included] an article that at first sounded serious enough in its title

> to divert me to it. [I thought I might] want to print it for use in future product liability cases. Its title was something like "The Steering Propensities of Pickup Trucks at Highway Speeds." As I read the article, I quickly learned that the author had written the three-page paper as a (poor) joke to describe how a pickup has become "the only beer-guided vehicle in the country," how pickups stall in front of bars, how to balance a beer to keep it from spilling in the crotch, et cetera. ■

Pittman's use of the Net to easily find information that he could then use to demonstrate to the court the strength of his arguments perfectly demonstrates the Net's great strength. Because the Internet enables virtually anyone to publish material for the world to see, it is a remarkably rich repository.

While professional researchers can take the time to search DIALOG or NEXIS to find pertinent articles, most people have neither the expertise to search those databases nor the desire to pay for access. In addition, such databases do not include articles written for fun. Online databases are generally collections of commercial publications, professional journals, and newsletters. While there is undeniable value in such collections, they also necessarily omit vast bodies of knowledge that, before the Internet, had little to no distribution.

Before the Net, Pittman may have been able to search DIALOG or NEXIS for published articles on the subject, or he may have sought to collect anecdotal information elsewhere, but it is unlikely he could have done either from the comfort of his office on the weekend, within a short period of time, for virtually no cost. The informal information he collected, which proved useful for defending his client, was available only from the unique library we know as the Net.

The Net is rich with free, valuable information that legal professionals and anyone else can conveniently access day or night. It offers an easy way to get smart fast about topics we may otherwise know nothing about. It's one thing to know the law on a given subject; it's another to be armed with the factual information required to make a winning argument.

### ■ SUCCESS STORY: ROBERT J. O'BRIEN

Solo practitioner Robert J. O'Brien of Buckhannon, West Virginia, relates how he used the Net to gather the facts he needed:

> Recently my juvenile client and I experienced a very bad result. My client was charged with violating a number of school rules, being sentenced to a residential facility for juvenile sexual offenders as a result of the recommendation of his counselor. Since the boy had not been even alleged to have committed any sexual offense during his two years on

probation, I have been concerned with researching the propriety of such a sentence, including recidivism rates for convicted sexual offenders and what kind of treatment is effective for sexual offenders.

With tips from counseling professionals, I found a number of sites, such as **http://www.northcoast.com/~dka/** [Delson-Kokish Associates], that provided me information that I can use in an upcoming reduction-of-sentence hearing. ■

O'Brien's online visit to Delson-Kokish Associates (DKA), a private counseling center located in Humboldt County, California—far from his West Virginia home—was made anonymously via the Net. He was able to benefit from some of the facts, definitions, and statistics provided by DKA. Without moving from his desk, O'Brien was able to pull up professionally prepared articles pertinent to the defense of his client, including the following:

- "Neglect—Our Biggest Child Abuse Problem—The One We Don't Want to Talk About"
- "Child Sexual Abuse—The Problem We Love to Talk About—But How Many Children Really Are Sexually Abused?"
- "Treatment for Victims and Perpetrators—What Works and What Doesn't Work—Hiding from Facts"
- "Why Adults Molest Children—'Are They Sick?'"
- "Treatment for Sex Offenders: Is It Worth Doing?"
- "Treating Sexually Abused Children: Does It Really Help?"
- "Child Protective Services—A Disappointing Record"
- "Repressed Memory—Agreement Between Adversaries"

## ■ SUCCESS STORY: DOUG HUMES

Doug Humes (**dhumes@voicenet.com**) practiced real estate and general corporate law for eleven years with the Reading Company (yes, the one on the Monopoly board). He then worked for four years with the Resolution Trust Corporation, selling off the pieces of the failed savings and loan industry. He now uses the Internet daily and relates here how he used it to search for a new job opportunity. (This originally appeared in the June 1996 edition of *The Internet Lawyer* newsletter [**http://www.internetlawyer.com**].)

Using the Internet as part of a job search strategy is not the sole province of the technogeeks. Anyone can incorporate the resources of the Internet into their job search, if they know where to look.

A friend recently sent me e-mail about a lawyer job advertised by a company called Shared Medical Systems. I first went to my home page collection of job resources (**http://www.voicenet.com/~dhumes**) [see Figure I.1] and clicked my link to the *Philadelphia Inquirer*'s classified sec-

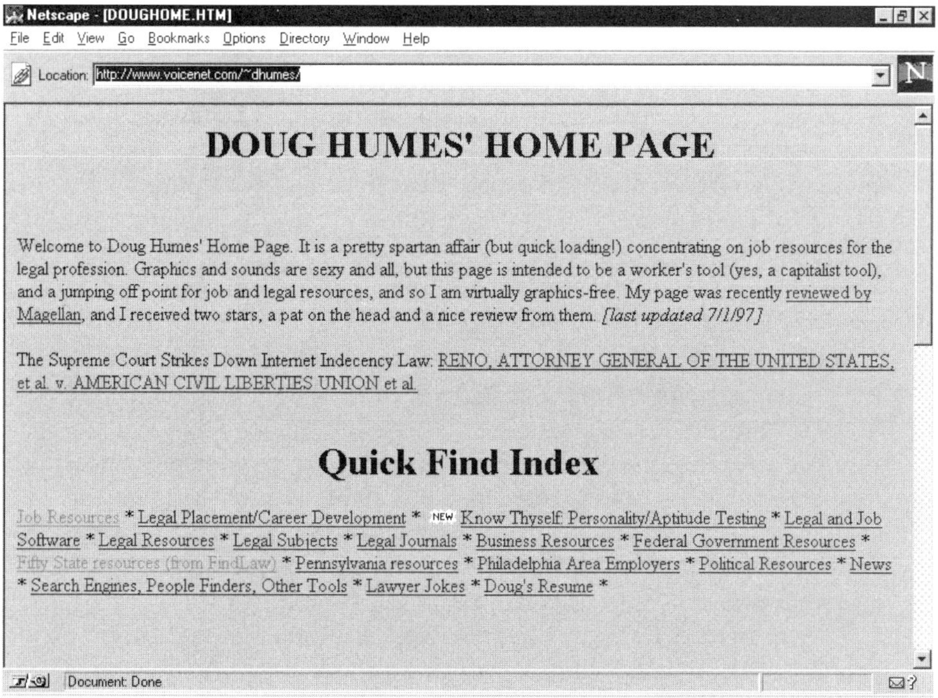


**FIGURE I.1.** Doug Humes's home page is chock full of job-search and other valuable (yet free) Internet resources.

tion (**http://www.phillynews.com/ads/**). Like many other newspapers (see Careerpaths at **http://www.careerpath.com** for six major metros), the *Inquirer* has virtually its whole newspaper online, with classifieds in a searchable database. I searched for *attorney* and quickly found the SMS ad.

To find out more about SMS, I first went to Hoover's Online corporate directory (**http://www.hoovers.com/bizreg.html**). Hoover's searchable directory returned four different links that would send me directly off to SMS information, including their latest stock quote, a stock chart for the last 100 days, a Web search using Infoseek, and their SEC filings. I followed each link in order. The first (from **http://www3.dbc.com/**) returned the stock quote information that you would find in the daily newspaper. The stock chart (from **http://quotes.galt.com/**) showed a leap in price from 39 to 60 between December and March. The Infoseek search (**http://guide-p.infoseek.com/**), using *Shared Medical Systems,* turned up a consultant who does business with them, but curiously (for a medical software company), no Web page for SMS.

The last source, SEC filings at EDGAR (**http://www.sec.gov/edgarhp.htm**), is one of the best resources on the Internet for finding information about publicly traded companies. At EDGAR I found the mother lode of information for SMS, including their 10-Ks and 10-Qs for the last several years. The problem here is that 10-Ks in particular are huge documents that take time to download. So I went back to my home page to pick up a helpful tool. At **http://worthnet.com/www/seczip/index.htm**, they will search EDGAR for you and then zip [digitally compress] your selections and e-mail them to you. I tried this out with the last 10-K and all 1995 10-Qs. I figured I would take a computer break and then come back in an hour and see if they had arrived, but first I checked my e-mail before logging out. Amazingly enough, the SEC documents were already in my mailbox. Once you receive them, you have to both uu-decode them and unzip them, but don't be intimidated here; this is knowledge that you are going to need to be fully functional in cyberspace anyway.

In the SEC reports, you get a great overview of the company, their financial statements, and for me most important, a list of their directors and officers. I use these with my network of contacts to see if they know any directors or officers, and so develop more information on the job and what person at SMS is actually doing the hiring.

I next went to Catapult's Business Site's list (**http://www.jobweb.org/CATAPULT/emplyer.htm**) and followed a link to Pathfinder (**http://pathfinder.com/@@Makgy9MMAgAAQJey/welcome/**), a collection of magazines and other documents that can be searched for your target. My search for *SMS* returned sixty documents, most of them entirely off subject or with a small mention of SMS buried many pages down. I found an SMS user's group and went to their site, where I was educated about SMS's new Invision product, and then found the link to the SMS home page. This really should have been my first stop, as they list career opportunities, product information, and press releases, among other things.

The SEC information had included SMS's general counsel, so my next stop was WESTLAW's searchable lawyer database (**http://www.wld.com/**). My search for the general counsel turned up no listing (not every lawyer is in there—it's voluntary). I then did a corporate search for Shared Medical and found their corporate listing. I learned that their legal department is between two and ten lawyers, and four attorneys are listed. Each listing includes law school and graduation date, and areas of concentration. The names of the attorneys provide me with more information for networking.

My final stop for the night was my favorite of all the Net resources: Switchboard (**http://www.switchboard.com/**). This is all the phone books for the country wrapped in one, plus more: a searchable database to find people and businesses. I put in the name of the general counsel of SMS, and up popped her home address and phone number. She lives in the next town over. I searched for the other attorneys and found the same information for two of four. This snooping for home addresses isn't a regular feature of my search, but you never know what information might give you a networking link to something else.

So after about an hour and a half on the Saturday that the ad first ran, I had a pretty good overview of the corporation, and the names of the influential people in the company to use in networking. This alone will not necessarily get me an interview or a job, but I am a few steps ahead of everyone else. That's the power of the Net in this Information Age: It gives you access to all of this information, in searchable form, from the privacy and comfort of your home computer. While nothing will replace your personal network as the best source for actually hearing about a job, the Internet gives you ready access to information that will better equip you to go after it. ■

## Other Uses of the Net

Several lawyers volunteered the following anecdotes describing how the Net is being used to solve research problems in law offices across the country. Bruce L. Dorner, who practices law in New Hampshire, relates these recent incidents:

> I had a client who was seriously injured in a propane explosion. I searched the Internet for references to propane. Once I filtered down to the better items, I found a link to the home page for the American Gas Association (http://www.aga.com/). They had all the standards of the industry posted, including comments about the particular appliance implicated in my case. Best of all, there was a phone number and an Internet mail address for further information. I got some good materials for the case.
>
> Another client wanted to adopt a child. A third party told him about a prospective birth mother in Tennessee, and my client thought this might be worth pursuing. My client needed the name of an attorney in Tennessee who handled interstate adoptions. A quick trip to West's Legal Directory (http://www.wld.com/) and a search using the phrase *interstate adoption* produced the information in just a few minutes.

Greg L. Siskind, Esq., of Siskind, Susser, Haas & Chang in Tennessee, explains how his firm uses the Net:

> [We use] the Internet for various nonlegal questions relating to our immigration cases, including
>
> - finding documentation to support human rights violation claims in connection with an asylum case (we actually found specific

references in an obscure UN document to the torture of our client by the government of Equatorial Guinea);

- [locating] expert witnesses for our cases;
- [getting] procedures sent to us by e-mail from officials at various U.S. consulates around the world;
- [submitting] "National Interest Waiver" green card applications that require a demonstration that the applicant's work will provide a substantial, prospective benefit to the United States. The key to winning these cases is documentation, and we often find articles and other support material on the Internet.

Michael C. Zusman, who practices commercial litigation with an emphasis on securities, real property, and creditors' rights, relates that one of his "partners was preparing to try a case involving an allegedly defective concrete floor laid by our client. One of the issues was whether the concrete was poured on a day where our client knew or should have known that the weather was too warm for the concrete to set properly. I hopped on my PC and, after linking around for a while, located a Web site for the Oregon Climatological Service (http://ocs.ats.orst.edu/) and obtained the name and e-mail address for our state climatologist, George Taylor. He responded, and I was able to obtain hour-by-hour temperatures for the relevant locality on the day in question, which, as I recall, my partner was able to introduce into evidence."

In a similar vein, Burgess Allison, a lawyer who works as a systems engineer at the MITRE corporation, reports that "the National Oceanic and Atmospheric Administration (NOAA) supports several hundred Web sites. I have been told that one of the largest groups of 'customers' for old weather data is lawyers . . . needing the weather stats for a particular location and date (usually associated with traffic accidents or some other mishap where visibility and weather conditions may have been a contributing factor)." For links to climatic data and historical data records, visit NOAA online (http://www.nws.noaa.gov/climate.shtml).

What is the advantage of using the Net? Why not just go to the library? Attorney Ted Claypoole answers these questions this way:

> Convenience and a broad general search to find what is out there. If I want to get a feel for what is going on in the area, I can sit down in the comfort of my own home and take an hour or two in the evening with the radio or TV on and do a general search and get some very good ideas of where I might want to go. I usually do not consider that a serious search. I still think it has advantages however. In other words, if I am online even once a week, and looking at legal topics, I will eventually know that Emory University has sixth circuit opinions—I bookmark

that, and the next time I want sixth circuit opinions and I am home and I want to word search them, I can go to that site. It just takes far more time than it is worth to actually say that "I am going to do all this research on the Web." You would spend way more time than you would need to. If you know where you are going already then it is a very good tool. If you do not know at all what is out there and you want to get an idea, it is a very good tool.

I think it is an exciting time for the Web. I had lunch with the editor of the business section of the local paper. He said he has gone to the Internet conference the last three years in Boston. He described it as—the first year was all Birkenstocks and beads and last year was all Armani suits and the money has started to flow into the Internet and it has started to become a valuable enough resource that over the next five to seven years, I think we will see a vast improvement in this resource as a research alternative.

# *PART* **ONE**

# *How to Conduct Research on the Net*

# CHAPTER ONE

# Thinking Like a Researcher

A GOOD RESEARCHER NEEDS TO BE A "FACT SLEUTH," someone who specializes in finding facts, in understanding why some facts cannot be found, and in figuring out whether any of the found facts are dependable. Surrounded by today's ocean of information, such detective skills are increasingly important. Lawyers and laypeople alike need to be able to pore through endless buckets of data to find the relevant drops. We are faced with so many data sources that simply keeping track of them, let alone vouching for their accuracy, can be overwhelming.

Effective use of the Internet for research depends on basic research skills and on understanding how to navigate the Net. It is a lot easier to find what you need quickly if you understand how information is compiled, accessed, and distributed, and how the structure of the Internet affects traditional approaches to research. To begin with, it is important to understand what research is and how the research process works.

## What Is Research?

Good researchers understand the subtle yet significant differences between three things: data, information, and knowledge. We use these terms so commonly that their individual meanings can easily be misunderstood. In fact, it is in combination that they provide us with a simple yet powerful definition of research. **Research** can be defined as the act of locating and organizing all pertinent pieces of data that comprise a body of information and then presenting this information in such a way as to enhance one's knowledge in a particular area. Each of the elements of research needs to be understood to fully comprehend what research is all about.

**Data** can be defined as individual facts and figures about people, places, and things, which can be found by any of us if we just ask around or look hard enough. Data is not hard to come by. In an age where communication is instantaneous and self-professed experts abound, it is not too difficult to have access to just about any piece of data we want, using just about any sources we need.

**Information** is what results when data is organized, collated, and accessible. In our common usage of the term, we have come to think of information as nothing more than an overwhelming collection of fact and myth, rumor and innuendo, misinformation and disinformation. We have thus managed to cast aspersions on information sources and on researchers themselves. If the messenger can ever be blamed for the message, then most professional researchers have, at some time or another, experienced firsthand such guilt by association. For this reason more than any other, the Information Revolution is now being overshadowed by a new period that many refer to as the Age of Knowledge. We can now say that we are no longer information-poor, but knowledge-challenged.

What the Information Revolution has ultimately provided is an environment where we now transport and shuttle more data back and forth amongst ourselves than we had ever dreamed possible, yet with only a limited certainty of just what to do with it all. This has also meant that traditional boundaries have blurred, making it even harder to distinguish between the key elements of basic research.

**Knowledge** derives from understanding what information may be needed when, what sources are most valid for obtaining it, and what should be done with it once we have found it. Only good research can facilitate the acquisition of this knowledge, and it is the wise knowledge seeker who appreciates the value of good research. By the same token, effective use of the Internet for any type of fact-finding that facilitates this process can be accomplished only by using it with the mind-set of a researcher.

## *Everyone Is a Researcher*

Traditionally, professional researchers have been trained to find information. Whether as librarians expected to manage ever-growing collections, or as academics who know which esoteric sources to consult to satisfy specific needs, researchers have typically served as information navigators, pointing knowledge seekers in the right direction to achieve certain goals.

The Information Revolution, however, has cultivated an increasingly dense data jungle, daunting to even the most skilled professional researchers. The exponential increase in sources and media has greatly complicated the task of finding information. Research has progressed from identifying relevant sources to requiring a continual alertness to new data opportunities and a heightened awareness that not all sources are equally trustworthy.

Additionally, the profile of the professional researcher has evolved from the trained specialist to include virtually everyone. Easy access to information that previously was available only to the cognoscenti or to those privileged with entrée to specialized data archives has created a responsibility to exercise that access. It is incumbent on every legal professional and every working person to be aware of the most cost- and time-effective means for retrieving the information necessary to get the job done. Competitive times require nothing less.

The role of researcher has been redefined to include professionals from all walks of life. From the classroom to the boardroom, good research skills have become necessary for everyone involved in obtaining or communicating information. Without an understanding of how research is typically done, it is unlikely that those who need to be informed will be able to obtain the quality of information they need.

No current development better illustrates this phenomenon than the Internet itself. With its intricate weaving of data sources, information providers, soothsayers, apostles, and advisors, the Internet forces users in the nonresearch community to face a sort of information future shock not unlike what the research community has seen evolving for many decades.

While information navigation skills are typically honed over a period of years, the Internet user is able to get up to speed in a relatively short time. More often than not, the common traps and pitfalls the occasional Internet user stumbles on can be avoided by mastering just a few key research navigation skills.

## Research Principles

There are essentially three key tenets of research technique. The first tenet is simple: Know what is out there before you try to find it. Even the Internet, with all of its high-tech wizardry, cannot teach us how to search for research ingredients. Research cannot be viewed as finding information so much as knowing where to look for it. Such knowing is the most effective way of avoiding wasted time (and money) on cyberwandering.

Once we locate the sources we need, we then must use them, which can easily become overwhelming. Sources can seem too voluminous to search, too complicated to use, or too filled with seemingly contradictory information. This is equally true in the print and electronic worlds. There is plenty of stuff out there; it is just hard to know what to do with it all.

This leads to the second tenet of sound research technique: The best sources of information are useless if you cannot get out of them what you need. We have all learned at some point that just because we can organize our intellectual attics, that doesn't mean that what is in there is any more valuable than when it was strewn all over the place. It just looks nicer.

There is an adage in accounting that states "Figures don't lie, but liars figure." The computer expert version is "Garbage in, garbage out." For most researchers, the maxim can be stated even more simply: "Just because it's published, doesn't mean it's true." Regular users of the Internet will recognize this sentiment. The Net puts the means of instantaneous worldwide publication at everyone's fingertips, from established commercial publishers to schoolchildren. Therefore, until its accuracy has been verified, data retrieved from the Internet must be viewed with skepticism—as must all information from any source.

This is the third tenet of information detective work: A healthy ounce of skepticism is worth a pound of information. Any good information gatherer can access data sources. But if we are after genuine knowledge, only quality research can create value from that data.

## Mastering the Research Mix

The seductive aura of the Internet has clouded its value for research of any depth or detail. The real research gems become hidden behind all of the bells, whistles, and gimmicks. The basic hurdle to Internet use is illustrated by the image of the World Wide Web as a spidery entanglement that we suspect might be worth using if we could just manage to find our way through it. This image can dismay even the sturdiest researcher as Web site after Web site begins to resemble an unmarked road. "Come into my Web site," says the network to the novice user. Too many Internet users end up feeling like entangled flies, when all they really need is a healthy dose of research savvy.

In the world of information sources, it is just as important to know the lay of the land as it is to find your way through it. This task has grown more daunting than ever with the advent of the Internet. Researchers have always had to face the challenge of keeping track of their sources, monitoring them, and being aware of their inherent worth. This task became even more challenging when the Information Revolution provided us with an ever-increasing number of sources and formats.

The growth of electronic information networks, of which the Net is the supreme example, has served to complicate the research process even while enhancing it. It has, at least on the surface, muddied the research waters a great deal, and it has made it more challenging to navigate what is known as the research mix, the fluid aggregate of information sources.

The research mix consists of both tools and techniques. The tools are identifiable sources of information that come in many packages. These packages can be people, places, and things. The techniques include being aware of these sources, having an appreciation of their inherent worth, and being able to work with the data found in them. Capitalizing on the research mix results from practicing good research skills. It consists of a keen familiarity with both sources and their use, and it can occur only when we have mastered the five key components of good research.

Foremost is (1) an understanding of just what we are looking for, followed by (2) an appreciation of why it is needed and how it will be used. Once these two have been established, we need to be aware of (3) where this information can be found (simultaneously considering the appropriateness and the availability of the sources) and (4) how it can be extracted. The final component of meaningful research is (5) knowing what to do with this information once we have accumulated it, so that it may in turn be converted into a body of knowledge.

As an example, say we have been asked to research why a particular computer software product was not successful. It would be easy to invest a significant amount of valuable research time examining how software design is benchmarked and how performance is measured. We might consult with academic instructors or professional associations and comb through texts and trade journals to determine common pitfalls of software programming. We might even trace the market history of the product manufacturer in question, trying to ascertain a proclivity for jumping the gun on product rollout with minimal quality assurance. Assuming our goal is to autopsy design efficiency and functional failure, this is a logical approach.

If, on the other hand, the intent of the research is to ascertain evidence of negligent product design that resulted in injury to the purchaser, then we would surely have been wasting our time. Herein lies the single most dangerous trap a researcher can fall into. Without a clear understanding of the purpose of the research—the end use—we are wasting time.

Capitalizing on the research mix is a lot like political campaigning. One needs to keep track of and stay up-to-date on everything and everyone likely to be of value. To effectively use the mix, the challenge is not just knowing how and where to find what you need. A good researcher must consider the availability of the data desired, the nature of the information offered, and the likelihood of obtaining it given the limitations of time and expense. This might involve the optimal use of existing resources, but it can often include taking a gamble every now and then on whether or not to continue pursuing what might very well be a dead end.

This is where mastering the research mix can become even more of a challenge, because we find we are not just testing our knowledge of sources and tools; we are also carefully weighing when and how to use them most efficiently. We are, in effect, balancing both substance and style. We are reinforcing our skills in using sources and in leveraging their use.

## *Using the Research Compass*

There are a great many benefits to using electronic sources when conducting research. There are also a great many challenges facing the researcher, not limited merely to technological concerns. No matter how well developed a software program is, no matter how fancy a Web page, and no matter how many pixels behind a monitor display, the online researcher is still unable to spread over the desktop the many different sources he or she is using. He or she cannot examine, compare, and jot notes on them.

This is not to say that electronic research sources cannot compare to print sources. It simply means one has to learn to think differently when using them, and this thinking usually needs to be done quickly and accurately. To maintain a focused and stable course of research, the professional researcher maintains a navigational reference point of sorts, much like the center of an equilateral triangle.

It is important to recognize the three sides of this research triangle: (1) the types of sources available (primary, secondary, and tertiary); (2) the economics of these sources (their format, availability, and ease of use); and (3) the validity of these sources (just how believable are they?). Successfully juggling all three of these components is the challenge facing anyone conducting research. Staying in the center of this triangle becomes even more critical when connected to an online source. When you can consistently keep the focus on what it is you are looking for, how and where you can most efficiently get it, and who or what would be the most appropriate sources to consult, then you are mastering the research mix and staying in the center of the triangle. Generally speaking, this will allow you to do a more effective job.

These key concepts are challenging enough to a researcher and have typically been considered independently from each other. The dynamics of the Internet, however, provide an environment that necessitates the simultaneous consideration of all of them. Making an effort to avoid going down the blind alleys of the Web, to strategically schedule Internet use based on factors such as time of day and data communications technology, and to decipher cryptic source messages in an often unmoderated environment are only some of the unique challenges facing the Internet user. Dealing with these peculiarities can either make or break an Internet researcher and will ultimately make the difference between using the Net effectively and just wasting time. Conducting research can sometimes be a lot like sailing uncharted seas, and this metaphor is particularly apt when attempting to surf the Internet.

As a researcher, what sets you apart from other information users is your ability to use the research compass, the navigational device that resides inside of the triangle. Not unlike a navigator's sextant or a builder's level, the research compass continually reminds you where you are, where you should be going, and how you can get there. Unlike mechanical instruments, though, the research compass is an internal measuring device. It is the research equivalent of a stockbroker's market timing or a sailor's feel for the rudder. You cannot necessarily quantify it, but you clearly know when you are using it.

When working optimally, the research compass serves as a beacon through the research mix. It allows you to get out of your own way, to zig when you were expecting to zag, and to hedge your bets when you are facing the crunch of a deadline. Ultimately, the purpose of the research compass is to help the knowledge navigator stay the course of the research mix and remain clearly focused within the research triangle. Using it effectively is by far the most meaningful skill a researcher can have.

# CHAPTER TWO

# Research Sources

KNOWING HOW TO CONDUCT RESEARCH includes recognizing the variety of available resources. Legal and general-interest researchers have different definitions for source categories, which are identified as *primary, secondary,* and, in the case of general research, *tertiary* sources.

To the legal researcher, primary research resources are sources of law—compilations of legislation, regulations, and court opinions. Such sources include state and federal statutory codes, the Code of Federal Regulations, and case law (court opinion) books and databases. Secondary sources, again in the legal context, are materials that discuss, illuminate, or otherwise provide reference to primary materials. Examples include treatises that may provide narrative overviews of an area of law, including references to relevant case law and statutes. A copyright treatise might discuss current copyright law, explaining recent court opinions that have interpreted the relevant statutes. Other legal secondary sources include law journals, legislative committee hearing transcripts, and indexes, which again provide commentary, explanation, and guidance to the law, but not necessarily access to the full text of statutes and case law.

To the professional researcher whose expertise cuts across any number of disciplines, primary and secondary sources have very different meanings. For example, secondary sources are generally the places to start conducting non-legal-specific research, because they can provide subject overviews and leads to other sources. The *Boston Globe* (http://www.boston.com/globe/) is such a secondary source that provides all sorts of subject coverage.

Say I am researching e-mail privacy. I start by conducting a quick search of the *Globe*'s Internet archive (dating back fifteen years) and find an article that is full of good information. The article quotes Mike Godwin of the Electronic Frontier Foundation and references an article on informational privacy in the *Santa Clara Computer and High Technology Law Journal*. The Godwin and journal references are tertiary sources, because they were referenced in a secondary source. If I call up Mike Godwin and interview him, he becomes a primary source of information. Further explanation of these various types of sources follows.

## *Primary Sources*

Primary source data is usually obtained from experts or specialists in some unique field or specialty area, and it is usually available only from them. These experts or specialists are typically people or organizations that have a recognized qualification to offer whatever information a researcher is looking for, and that can be expected to know about new or groundbreaking developments in a particular area because of their expertise in it.

Consulting with primary sources can sometimes be referred to as getting information straight from the horse's mouth. With the advent of the Internet and related technologies for information delivery, there are now many more such horses that a researcher can approach in the search for accurate information. Good research skills enable distinguishing between the thoroughbreds and the also-rans.

Primary research sources can be dynamic or static. They can quell rumors or speculation about current or esoteric information, or they can provide expert confirmation that something undocumented may be true. More than any other type of research source, the Internet has magnified the value of primary research data and, through the Net's massively broad distribution mechanism, made both the use of and access to primary sources easier than ever.

Depending on the nature of the data, the holders of primary information may deem it worthy of being saved for posterity, or they may simply file it mentally. When the latter occurs, primary research data can resurface in the form of tertiary information (more on this in a moment). But when the information is deemed worthy of preservation, it will usually be transcribed into print or electronic form for either proprietary or public consumption. If it is proprietary, meaning it is viewable only by select individuals, its value to the researcher is limited (in direct proportion to its accessibility).

Such proprietary data may be available for a price, or only if the requester fits some particular profile. At other times, it may be of such a highly confidential nature that it cannot be released to anyone outside a specified group.

With reference to research information sources, researchers have sometimes said, "If you can't see it or touch it, but you know it's there, it's probably primary data." This is largely because primary data has historically been something obtained by conducting in-person interviews, listening to taped recordings of speeches or commentaries, or requesting permission to view some piece of unique documentation not available anywhere else. The point is that the information was not that easy to obtain. The Internet has changed that.

Time and money, more than actual availability, have historically been the factors limiting our ability to use primary research data. Knowing some nugget of knowledge exists, but not in any quantified available form, is far more frustrating than discovering that something you thought was true is not.

## *Creating Primary Data*

No matter how valuable it may be to the research at hand, if the data you need is unavailable, it cannot be used. At such times, the research compass should kick in, to navigate toward another point in the research mix, to expedite the research process. Alternatively, there is a research technique that prevails over the limitation of existing data sources. It is less subject to time and money concerns because it is focused on obtaining that essential piece of knowledge that is dangling like a brass ring, just out of reach.

In the tradition of investigative journalists and competitive intelligence professionals, the researcher who really needs information will go find it. Just because information has not been published or otherwise documented does not mean that you cannot establish and verify facts and transcribe them into a form that will serve the needs of your research. This process may involve locating former employees of a particular company to interview them concerning employee grievance policies during a particular time period. Or it might involve hiring a private investigator to document the whereabouts of an individual who has otherwise disappeared. Essentially, any information out there can be obtained if you try hard enough. These techniques, however, should not be mistaken for primary research as defined in traditional information circles. For our purposes, primary information is source data that is neither classified nor confidential, but merely limited in availability and generally not published in publicly available sources.

## Secondary Sources

Once research data is compiled, organized, and distributed publicly for mass consumption, we usually refer to it as secondary information because it is no longer under the control of restricting caretakers. Secondary sources generally comprise the bulk of material used in day-to-day research. It is voluminous, to say the least, and growing in supply at a fantastic rate.

Secondary source information can consist of what we immediately see in a library or research center as we walk in. It is made up of books, newspapers, magazines, journals, published papers, public speeches, directories, reference guides, and almanacs (to name just a few). Secondary data sources also include electronic formats of all of these materials (whether optical, magnetic, or available via online distribution). Electronic media have become so prevalent that some secondary sources are published exclusively in electronic form. Whether it is sold or distributed free of charge, secondary information is, by nature, available to anyone familiar with the means for obtaining it.

At the heart of secondary source access is the belief that the knowledge seeker does not need to meet any unreasonable criteria for use of the information. Of course, the key here is what constitutes "unreasonable." While there may be guidelines or conditions to be enforced (such as access or subscription fees, or copyright adherence), secondary source users need not meet any personal qualifications. Other than the ability to understand the data presented, there is no real limitation to a researcher's ability to capitalize on secondary sources.

Such understanding, though, is no minor qualification. Experienced researchers are increasingly proving their value to information seekers not merely in their expertise at using sources but also in knowing the hoops one must jump through to get to them. When it comes to maximizing the potential of secondary sources in the Information Age, skilled researchers must be intimately familiar with the protocols, restrictions, and regulations governing their use. Today it is not enough to be able to pull a rabbit out of a hat when conducting research; one needs to be well versed in the art of hat selection as well.

This is especially true when conducting fact-finding research on the Internet. Unlike an organized library or information research center, the Internet is more like a flea market of data sources, and we are continually challenged to bob and weave and select carefully. The expert researcher knows how to determine which sources can be trusted, for the principle of caveat emptor goes with the territory in research. Distinguishing the outstanding and unique sources from the suspect is a critical research skill when using the Internet or any resource on which you depend.

## *Tertiary Sources*

Effectively using primary and secondary source information can arguably be the only real methodology a good researcher needs to perform adequately. As with fine-tuning an instrument or mastering an athletic technique, however, knowing how to finesse research defines the real pro. For example, those engaged in ongoing research need to recognize the role that tertiary information sources can play, and how these sources can subtly direct us toward research treasures.

In simplest terms, tertiary sources can be described as whatever else we think of using in conducting research. Tertiary information is revealed every time we are referred to alternative sources of information, either by secondary or primary sources or by word of mouth. We may be interested in a bibliographical footnote, a white paper inserted into a trade journal, or something alluded to or hidden in a related source. Similarly, a thought or a comment made to us by another person might trigger an idea or point us up some avenue not previously considered.

Even researchers themselves can serve as effective tertiary sources. In conducting research in a particular area over time, experienced researchers can spot the trends, the hidden messages, and the credibility of information sources so effectively that their research compasses are more refined and self-directed than those of less experienced researchers. Such experts are very good at developing hunches and following leads that can be easily overlooked in the bustle of day-to-day research. Their comprehensive knowledge of sources and source accessibility provides a tertiary research value that cannot be quantified, though it is high in quality.

For example, say we are continuing the research begun in the first chapter, concerning why a computer software product was not successful. We happen to come across a reference in a trade journal article to a recently held trade show focusing on small home offices and telecommuting. The article quotes by name, or includes in a bibliography, a person or group known to be prolific in this area of research. With due consideration of the time available for our research, we might contact the organization responsible for coordinating the conference, or contact by phone or electronic mail the authorities included in the bibliography. Whether or not we turn up a research gem, we have just used a tertiary research technique. It is somewhat like taking a wrong turn in a strange city; we may or may not end up enjoying the experience. A good researcher, however, is usually quite skilled at sensing ahead of time whether or not such "wrong turns" are likely to be worth the effort.

While tertiary data can easily fall through the cracks of the research process or even be written off as superfluous when they do not meet an immediate need, such data can alternatively provide the seeds necessary for follow-up research or the leads needed for future primary research. Consider, for example, the bibliography or interviews cited in the trade journal article, or even the summary of the previously unknown trade show. Sometime down the road, it is quite likely we will be thankful to have made mental note of them. Should we ever need to track down expert sources for more-detailed primary research, we will save a lot of research shoe leather by knowing whether or not to begin there on our next research journey.

Unlike the use of primary or secondary sources, the use of tertiary sources usually occurs unintentionally. Like some subconscious stimulant, tertiary information can work as a sort of bookmark in the research process, reminding us that there are additional quadrants on the research map we may wish to explore at a later time.

Indeed, the bookmark technology built into World Wide Web browser software encourages the use of tertiary sources. It is easy to pull down a list of links gathered while surfing the Web and then click over to, for example, the Software Publishers Association (http://www.spa.org/) to peruse the archives. The single biggest frustration in using tertiary information has always been, When will I ever know if I want to use this or not? With Web bookmarks, you can put something aside for future reference and never have to worry about locating it again when you actually need it.

# *CHAPTER* **THREE**

# ***Research Methodology***

BOTH TRADITIONAL AND UNUSUAL RESEARCH APPROACHES are called for when moving through the Internet, to reach the substantial sources that will answer research questions. It is worthwhile to understand the research tools available and to learn professional tricks of the trade, to avoid online frustration. By mastering the range of Internet sources and content and by recognizing how to ensure the accuracy and comprehensiveness of sources, it is possible to turn Internet use into a very rewarding experience.

## ***Selecting Research Sources***

"Know your sources!" is an often overlooked, yet essential principle for good business researchers, journalists, and lawyers to follow. Faced with the bountiful hybrid of print and electronic media, those engaged in research need to understand that this principle applies equally to both the content and the providers of information sources.

Knowing *what* source to use *when* is at the core of any serious research. Simply finding the required data is only half the battle. Data must become attributable to gain value. Whether attributable to a verbal, print, or other type of source, the data must also be what you were after in the first place to be useful to the research at hand. Finally, optimal value is achieved when the researcher can take information attributable to some source and add a personal spin by qualifying or making inferences based on that source.

The research source category—primary, secondary, or tertiary—indicates a source's proximity to the genesis of information. The category of each source can also tell a researcher just how hot certain information is, and just how much it can be believed. Information sources need to be examined with the same care and skepticism as information itself to achieve maximum research value.

Consider an example that illustrates how researchers continually need to keep these distinctions in mind. Suppose we were asked to conduct research comparing the use of computers in the home and computers in business. Before tackling an assignment of this magnitude, we ought to make sure we understand the phrase "use of computers in the home and in business." In this way, we can identify some research directions and establish some questions for our research to answer.

It would really simplify the research process if we could just go to the source article titled "The Use of Computers in Homes and Businesses," but this article is not likely to exist. If a researcher happened to find such a source, a skeptical eyebrow ought to rise before the source is relied on too heavily. A source that precisely responds to so unique and broad a research request is rare. The likelihood is that it may respond in some way, but not comprehensively, to the questions raised.

One of the first lessons a researcher learns is that an information request must be examined and restated more than once to remove ambiguity and misdirection. To paraphrase Yogi Berra, "Know where you're going, or when you get there, you'll be lost." Missing this step, more than any other, can lead to a significant waste of research time and money and send the researcher scurrying into oblivion. Such oversights underscore the importance of quality research skills.

Clearly stated objectives and an agreed-upon understanding of the goals of the research at hand will help prevent miscues, missteps, and headaches along the way. In keeping with the research compass metaphor, a smart navigator charts the course well before embarking. That may mean narrowing the scope of the research request and determining the end use or reason for the research. To avoid errors in judgment, we ought to ask for a number of clarifications before proceeding to research.

For example, we might ask, What types of computers are relevant? Desktop computers or workstations? Personal computers or mainframes? Computers on networks or stand-alone computers? We need to understand what is meant by "use." Are we discussing software or hardware applications? Do we mean business or recreational/educational use at home? Any one of these reduced questions would be a substantial research topic by itself. Combined, they can become so unwieldy that we would be unlikely to find sufficient answers in the allotted time. At best, we would end up supplying one of the most dreaded research results: the overwhelming information dump. Such an undigested pile of articles, citations, and signposts to other sources and bits of information might lead to a coherent result, if one took the time to plow through it. Or it might not. In any case, the information dump in itself is not a responsive research result.

Only when the focus of research is adequately narrowed and the sources most likely to lead to meaningful results are known, only then should research begin. Knowing precisely which research destinations are best is what separates the expert from the beginner. In the context of comparing computer use in the home and the workplace, there are likely countless secondary sources available: magazine articles, newspaper features, even academic textbooks. And what of quantitative data? What if we need to get access to numbers, statistics, hard figures? There might well be some very valuable pieces of primary data indicating, for example, how many computers the major manufacturers have sold into the home market. Some of this information might be proprietary or confidential, and some may be available to the public. The accomplished researcher will think of legitimate, creative ways to gain access to it.

For example, primary data might include membership surveys of computer user groups or clubs. Trade associations often compile industry statistics that are available to their members or to outsiders for a small fee. It might even be worthwhile to interview an industry specialist who may be widely known as a speaker or writer. Such an individual can often add the valuable perspective of one who has been researching the topic for years and analyzing trends independently.

In each instance, the experienced researcher should be able to rise to the challenge and provide substantive, responsive data. What sets a good researcher apart from a merely adequate researcher is being able to gain access to particularly tough-to-find data in particularly hard-to-reach sources that are particularly reputable. Some of the advantages of supplementing the more easily located secondary data with the harder-to-find primary data include timeliness, qualification, and newsworthiness. It also demonstrates that a special effort has been made to provide high-quality and appropriately comprehensive research service.

All sources of research data, whether primary, secondary, or tertiary, are of value only when used effectively. The best time to use a source is dictated equally by accessibility, immediacy of need, and available research time. The best way to use a source is, unfortunately, determined primarily through experience in using it. What this has most often meant for researchers is that time spent in libraries provides the skills necessary to cut through confusing sources. The savvy to know when to use which source, and just how much faith to have in each, comes primarily from spending many years trying to balance source usefulness against source credibility and from falling flat after making mistakes. Success comes from trying again despite failure.

The arrival of essentially free, widely accessible Internet research capabilities has put so many data sources at the fingertips of so many that beginners have been known to burst out with, "Look at how much I've got here!" But as anyone who has ventured onto the Web without a good research framework knows, the ocean of sources can be a curse as well as a blessing. Although search engines like Infoseek and AltaVista and subject indexes like Yahoo do enable keyword searching of the Web, they do not provide the quality of organization we have become accustomed to thanks to card catalogs and librarians. One cannot accomplish in one Internet session the sort of high-quality research that requires basic research skills, without honing such skills over years of experience.

## Evaluating Research Sources

In addition to knowing how to approach research from a navigational standpoint, good research skills involve knowing which tools to pick up. While trained researchers are well schooled in finding information, their research cunning is truly demonstrated only if the right sources are chosen.

Just as a methodology exists for evaluating how a researcher thinks, a similar methodology exists for evaluating what a researcher uses in conducting research. Professional researchers know the difference between primary, secondary, and tertiary research sources. While the Internet has not changed the distinction between such sources, it definitely has changed the best places to look for them.

The Internet's most dramatic contribution in terms of sources involves easier locating of primary sources and increased limitations on secondary sources. As to tertiary sources, the Net has had little effect on whether or how these alternative sources are used. It has, however, made it easier to monitor them.

In the past, the need to track down a primary source slowed research down. The key factors influencing the completion of research were generally time and source availability, not necessarily the accumulation of the required data or information. The rise of the Internet has inverted this principle. It can be difficult for experienced researchers to adjust to an environment where the primary source—the needle in the haystack—is the first target, and secondary sources are left for later.

There is a distinct methodology researchers use in trying to decide what types of sources to use and when, which is akin to the research compass and the research mix. A good researcher knows how to balance the importance of the target information against both the availability of sources and the time and expense involved in using them. Whether or not to then jump on the Net becomes the next critical decision the researcher faces.

Consider first the most common research sources. In the print medium, the common sources are easily available, provided one has some sort of library access. The costs of such print materials are typically not borne by the researcher. Rather, the source licensing fee has already been absorbed by the library. The Internet researcher needs to know that while many sources are available free online, they are not all free. Sometimes, it is more cost-effective to pull a book off a library shelf than it is to pay for it on the Net.

Some examples of such secondary sources are Gale's *Encyclopedia of Associations,* National Register Publishing Company's *Directory of Corporate Affiliations,* and *Value Line.* All of these illustrate secondary sources that, while containing valuable, frequently needed information, are rather expensive in hard copy. When using them in their print form, the researcher benefits a great deal from the library's willingness to provide them free of charge. At present, however, only Gale's *Encyclopedia of Associations* is available in full text on the Internet, and, as with all of the Net-converted Gale sources, prepayment is required (although, as Figure 3.1 shows, you will find a free demo at http://galenet.gale.com:8888/intro/demo/). You can find a description of the *Directory of Corporate Affiliations* at DIALOG's site (http://www.corp.dialog.com/dialog/databases/html2.0/bl0513.html).

There has been a rise in the number of information suppliers and publishers who have been either charging for online access to their publications or requiring online registration before permitting use. On the surface, this seems fair, considering that print subscribers to such sources typically must pay for use. On the other hand, Net precedents for free access have been set for a number of years. It is therefore understandable that many Internet researchers take exception to publishers' requests for payment simply to access popular sources.

Before the Web, which began to explode in 1995, the Internet was a bastion of primary research sources. These included museums and archives, societies and associations, and the frequently used discussion forums (newsgroups and listservs). Encouraged by the emergence of the Web as the most common way to access the Net, electronic publishing propelled graphical online document access to the fore. A typical initial

**FIGURE 3.1.** Gale's *Encyclopedia of Associations* is a useful secondary source available on the Internet for a fee.

response was, "Why should I buy the *New York Times* when I can read it on the Web for free?"

Those were the days. Such discoveries spread through the world of printed resources. Electronic versions of books, magazines, newspapers, and newsletters popped up all over the Internet landscape. This, in turn, led to another initiative that proved to be particularly valuable to the Internet researcher: electronically based publications.

These sources were unique in that they had no print equivalent anywhere and could be located only on the Net. They appeared initially at university locations in the form of refereed academic journals, which meant that their content was critiqued and verified by qualified researchers (see Figure 3.2). Electronic publications proved to be the vehicle whereby Internet information sources really proved their uniqueness. There were now clear-cut reasons why the Net should be used for research: It provided reliable, authoritative information that could not be found anywhere else. Even better, it didn't cost anything!

While many of the original Internet-only-based publications were refereed and edited, too many subsequent sources were not. This led to suspicions about the worth of the Internet as a research tool. While forward-

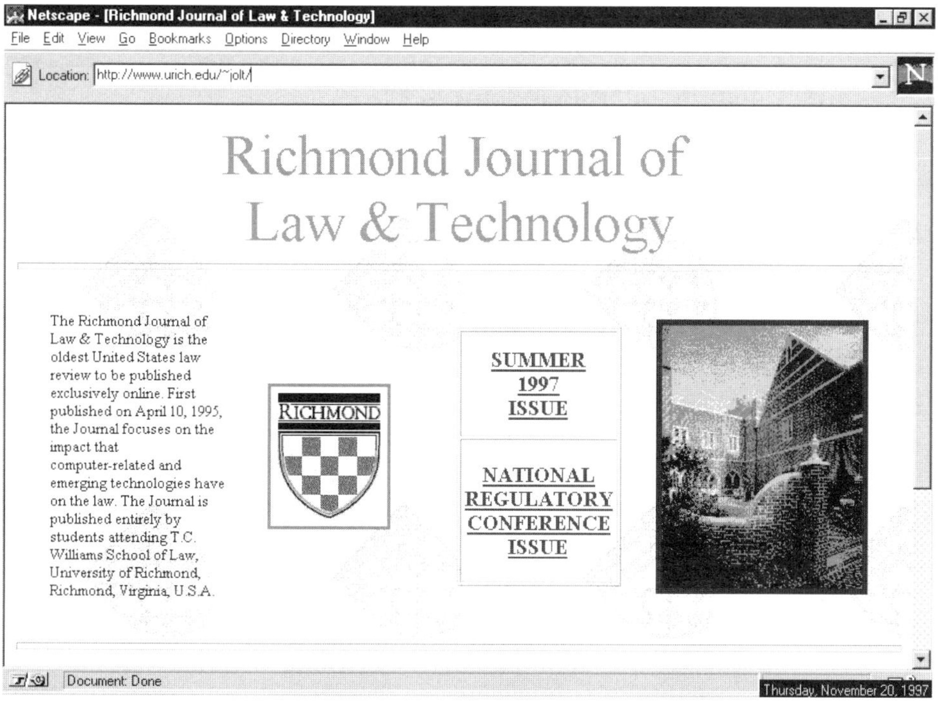


**FIGURE 3.2.** The *Richmond Journal of Law & Technology* (**http://www.urich.edu/~jolt/**) was the first law journal published exclusively online.

thinking publishing houses were successfully transitioning to the Internet, the so-called vanity press industry was following in its wake, and the lines of demarcation between them were becoming blurred, just as in the print world.

These lines became even more blurred as individuals and hobbyists began developing their own Web sites under the guise of some alleged subject expertise. The ease with which Net searchers can now inadvertently access sites of debatable value that may resemble something they are looking for has not helped any. Enthusiastic cries of "I can't believe what I found on the Net!" are giving way to more cynical cries of "Can you believe this stuff on the Net?"

More frustrating to the researcher has been good old free enterprise. Coupled with the increasing demand for Net- and Web-accessible secondary sources has been a decreasing willingness on the part of publishers to simply give things away for free. Again, the seemingly simplistic days of information-sharing altruism among Internet pioneers appears even more quaint as the industry side of the information industry has steamrolled through.

**ADDITIONAL RESOURCES FOR EVALUATING SOURCES**

Ten Cs for Evaluating Internet Resources

http://www.uwec.edu/Admin/Library/10cs.html

Thinking Critically about World Wide Web Resources

http://www.library.ucla.edu/libraries/college/instruct/critical.htm

## *Deciding When to Use the Net*

The researcher's judgment must remain sharp when determining whether to use the Net for fact-finding research. Maintaining an edge is a process of continually questioning oneself about source issues, as illustrated by the following Internet methodology checklist:

- What sources are needed to locate the data or information I need?
- What is the likelihood of finding these sources on the Net?
- How immediately can these sources be accessed elsewhere, if at all?
- What will it cost?
- Will I likely need to use these sources again?

While appearing to be painstaking at the outset, this thought process is crucial to the researcher, especially if there are limitations of time and expense. When well integrated into the research mix, this Net methodology checklist becomes second nature to the researcher and is often processed in no time. It is, in fact, not very different from the step-by-step approach employed by researchers for many years in the realm of print research. It is at the heart of truly effective Internet use and is mastered not simply by learning how to surf the Net like a pro, but by remembering to think like a researcher.

Knowing what sources are needed to locate research data is a skill picked up over time and nurtured each time research is conducted. It involves, for example, knowing that magazines or newsletters exist for most academic disciplines, that libraries and archives are good sources for historical data, and that there are basic differences between encyclopedias, almanacs, dictionaries, and directories.

This way of thinking about published resources can lead to a method for thinking about government offices, corporations, professional societies, and other such organizations. In this way, we can mentally catalog the fact that NOAA (the National Oceanic and Atmospheric Administration—http://www.ncdc.noaa.gov/) is a source of historical weather data, that the U.S. Department of Commerce provides historical trade data (http://www.ita.doc.gov/industry/otea/), and that the National Technical Information Service (http://www.fedworld.gov/) contains publicly available Department of Defense information.

Simply knowing that an organization or periodical has the information one needs, however, is not enough. One must find it on the Net, and this can be a challenge for the novice researcher. Nothing is more frustrating than knowing that a desired piece of data exists, but being unable to get to it. Although Internet search engines do an amazing job of collecting and keyword-searching millions of Web sites, the depth within those Web sites, where valuable data often lurks, can be harder to catalog and therefore harder to penetrate for the data you need (see Figure 3.3).

Relying on the popular search engines such as Lycos, Yahoo, or Infoseek is a lot like trying to find out who lives on Main Street by using a phone book of the world. The use of search engines often ought to be a last resort for Internet researchers, rather than a first choice. These search

**FIGURE 3.3.** The Library of Congress site is an outstanding example of an extremely deep site, chock full of information that is not necessarily easy to find without burrowing through the site itself.

tools take time and experience to master, and skilled researchers often depend more on human "wetware"—intuition and practiced hunches—before proceeding to use software search tools.

The likelihood of finding secondary sources on the Internet depends more on familiarity with traditional sources than on any innate Internet skill. Lack of such familiarity is one of the primary reasons time is lost while attempting to conduct research on the Net.

Table 3.1 offers a very simple list of source types. All of these are available in print and on the Internet. Knowing how accessible a resource is in other media (whether print, CD-ROM, or other form), before jumping online, can save lots of time. It has been said that the most valuable skill an Internet researcher can have is knowing when *not* to use the Net. If one is about to invest time in accessing, searching, and sifting through hyperlinked Internet sources, it ought to be worth the trip. There is no better testament to the lack of Internet value then having a colleague pull a copy of the *World Almanac* right off the shelf while you are hyperlinking through home pages, and then flip to the page with the data you are looking for in less than half the time.

If, on the other hand, an Internet surfer can verify the toxicity of an accidental overdose of an over-the-counter drug by accessing an online

**TABLE 3.1.** Basic data sources

| Desired Source | Common Formats |
|---|---|
| Primary Resource | |
| Hard-to-find expert data | Professional society or organization |
| | Academic research center |
| | Qualified individuals |
| Closely held business data | Public filings |
| | Market studies |
| | Corporate information centers |
| Secondary Resource | |
| Business and trade statistics | Almanacs |
| | Encyclopedias |
| | Directories |
| General-interest data | Magazines |
| | Newspapers |
| | Newsletters |

pharmaceutical encyclopedia that is not located on a nearby shelf (see Figure 3.4), then the Net as a research tool has more than proved its worth.

There are plenty of things to think about when choosing the format in which to access a source. For example, paying a service fee (to a research company, for example) to access data available only in print, rather than purchasing the entire print source, is worthwhile if the source is needed only rarely. If, on the other hand, a researcher finds that a regularly updated source is required frequently, it may be most efficient to subscribe to a paper update service via postal mail and access the information online only for the immediately needed latest issue.

These examples have all centered on the use of known sources, that is, secondary sources of information that the researcher is already familiar with. Where the Internet has really turned research principles upside down is in the area of primary research sources.

The thought process behind source selection remains the same for primary and secondary sources. Recognizing the option to consult with a

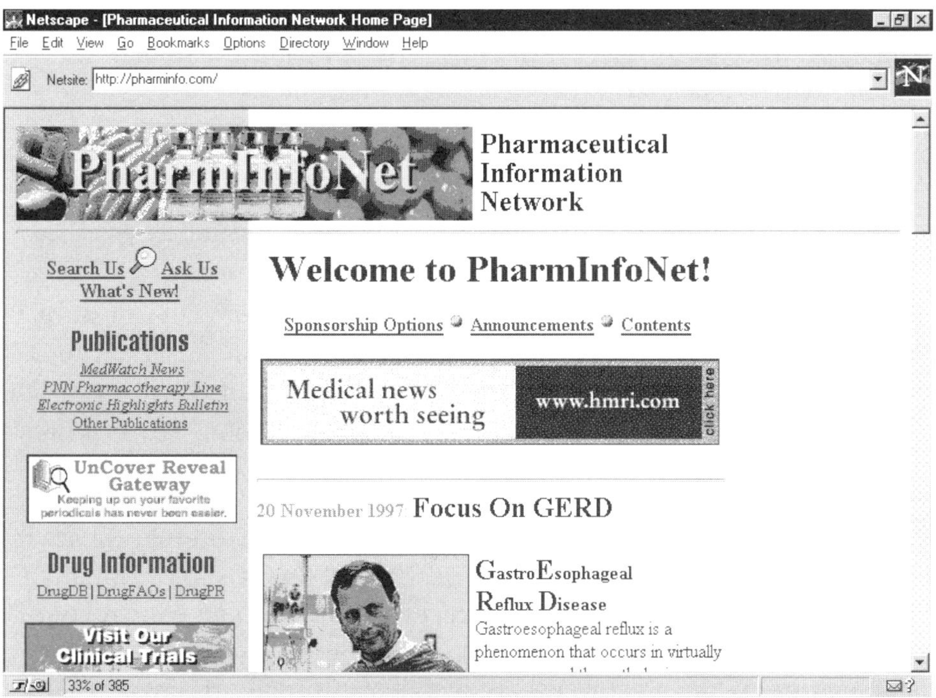


**FIGURE 3.4.** The Pharmaceutical Information Network provides assessments of therapeutics and advances in new drug development, including full-text articles from clinical publications and information from scientific meetings. A drug database is provided.

professional organization rather than a print source is a research skill developed regardless of the Internet. What the Net does is encourage use of primary sources. All the reasons not to call a particular association for an expert opinion evaporate when using the Net. When the researcher is pressed for time, for example, it is maddening to wait for a call back that may not arrive. This problem does not exist on the Net. Web sites never sleep.

The Internet is quite simply a revolutionary research tool, particularly in terms of providing access to primary resource data. There are two reasons for this. First, the ability to find unique individuals (for example, experts or a spectrum of people you may need to survey) is made far easier by the Net, which conveniently gathers people (via discussion forums, for example) into interest groupings. Using the Net, you can easily reach the folks who care about law enforcement as well as those who focus on the laws of gravity or virtually any other subject you can imagine. The Internet provides direct access to the people you need to reach for answers. It works quite easily. All you need to do is post a message to any of the tens of thousands of different newsgroups or mailing lists and then just wait a while. There are many ways to post to newsgroups, but one Web-accessible method is to use the posting mechanism at DejaNews (http://www.dejanews.com). (See Figure 3.5.) Generally, within the hour, your message will be automatically distributed to thousands of list recipients. It is very likely that several of them will respond with information you can use.

Keep in mind, though, before you post, that many discussion forums have codes of behavior, also known as acceptable-use policies. The best idea is to read through the forum a bit, before posting, so you get a sense of the sort of folks using the list and the behavioral norms they observe. If you fail to pay attention to these cultural quirks, you are less likely to receive useful responses to your postings, and in fact you may find yourself subject to the list users' ire in the form of nasty e-mail or, worse, a smudge on your firm's reputation.

Second, the millions of Web sites available virtually guarantee that you will find an organization's site, which may provide useful primary resource data. It is now a safe assumption that just about every company and professional society has a Web site, even if it is "under construction." Company sites are quite valuable for accessing corporate data and product literature. When all you need is overview information, the company site is a better bet than Securities and Exchange Commission public filings. Professional association sites are particularly useful for verifying personal credentials, for contact information (look in the membership di-

**FIGURE 3.5.** DejaNews makes it particularly easy to read and post to newsgroups.

rectories), or for accessing technical papers discussing industry-specific phenomena. The Net's powerful and unique research value becomes plain once you master accessing these primary sources.

Before examining some key fact-finding sources and strategies on the Net, let us review the key principles of our Internet methodology checklist.

### What Sources Are Needed to Locate the Data or Information I Need?

More than any other preparatory work in our research journey, this one consideration deserves a lot of attention right off the bat. The if-then reality check can work wonders here. *If* we are trying to track down a particular type of information, *then* right off the bat we should consider certain types of sources. Table 3.2 demonstrates this approach.

### What Is the Likelihood of Finding These Sources on the Net?

The ability to answer this question becomes a vital intuitiveness for the Internet researcher. In an environment where both sources and site locations can appear or disappear at any time, the likelihood of finding a given source on the Net can be the toughest thing to be certain of.

**TABLE 3.2.** The best sources for particular types of information.

| Information | Traditional Source Formats or Types |
|---|---|
| Expert data | Professional societies or organizations; archives or museums; academic libraries; trademarks or patents; conference proceedings; papers or dissertations |
| Company backgrounds | Directories and yearbooks; SEC filings; annual reports; press and news wires; newspapers, newsletters, and magazines |
| Personal biographical | Directories and yearbooks; almanacs; membership guides; press and news wires; newspapers, newsletters, and magazines; personal interviews |
| General-interest news | Newspapers and magazines; TV and radio news footage and tapes |
| Esoteric, niche data | Almanacs and yearbooks; encyclopedias and dictionaries; archives and museums; clubs and user groups; personal interviews |

Sources that you used yesterday could be gone tomorrow, and sources that never existed before suddenly spring up everywhere, like dandelions. Experienced researchers learn to check regularly for developments so they will not be taken by surprise when a needed resource is missing, and so they will know when a new treasure trove is online.

These discoveries can make Internet research very rewarding. Experienced researchers learn to grasp certain patterns about Internet sources, and these patterns, while not absolute truths, constitute a pretty dependable research compass. Here are a few of these standards of Internet use:

- Nearly every company worth its salt has a Web site.
- The same holds true for colleges, universities, and trade organizations.
- Anything you subscribe to for a fee will eventually be available online in full text.
- For the most part, entire books (such as almanacs, dictionaries, encyclopedias, and so forth) have not yet made it online to the extent that subscription-based periodical publications have.
- You can find an Internet discussion group for just about anything under the sun.

Keeping these points in mind during all stages of the research process can save you a lot of time when you embark on Internet research. If one invests enough time in considering what types of sources are needed to find a particular piece of information, a lot of wasted time and effort can be avoided. Similarly, the research experience will be far more rewarding and enjoyable if one begins by saying, "Okay, I'm going to need to find a nonprofit organization on the Net" or "If I can just get to company XYZ's site" or "I'll bet that so-and-so's Web site will have some useful related links, and I can avoid those darn search engines!"

### How Immediately Can These Sources Be Accessed Elsewhere, If at All?

On the surface, this could be viewed as an argument against using the Net for research. How can one maximize Internet research skills by thinking of other places to look, foregoing the Net altogether? The point here is that the Net is a tool to assist us in conducting research, not an end in itself. Using the Net when one can more efficiently get what is needed somewhere else is a lot like banging a nail with a screwdriver. Overlooking these considerations leads to the kinds of Internet headaches that contribute to its undeserved reputation as a waste of time.

A good rule of thumb for the Internet researcher is this: The more generally or commonly known a piece of information is likely to be, the easier it might be to locate it somewhere other than on the Net. Conversely, the more challenging your research quandary, the more you might want to consider grabbing your surfboard and logging on.

### What Will It Cost?

This is one of those caveats that was almost unheard of in the world of Internet research some ten to twenty years ago. Today, an Internet researcher would do well to keep track (either mentally or in a journal) of those sources that have begun charging user or registration fees, or at least giving signs of doing so. When time is of the essence (such as when faced with a tight deadline) or when involved in a high-profile money-is-no-object research assignment, using a fee-based Internet source may not be so critical an issue.

If, on the other hand, there is time to spare or if expenses must be kept to a minimum, flipping through the pages of the *New York Times* or the *Wall Street Journal* by hand can be far more productive for the researcher. Furthermore, although some sources may tout themselves as having no-fee availability on the Internet, researchers should beware certain signs. For example, it cannot be assumed that "full text on the Internet" necessarily means "complete text on the Internet." Because of the economics of data storage and telecommunications technology, many information providers have been forced to convert their data sources selectively, rather than fully, into electronic format. This practice has been in place in the world of online bibliographic databases for many years.

Hence, it is possible that a piece of data available in some non-Internet version of a source may not turn up on the Internet or other electronic services. This is understandable, and experienced researchers will keep their eyes peeled for such discrepancies. Over time, such savvy proves quite helpful in deciding when, and if, to go fact finding on the Net.

### Will I Likely Need to Use These Sources Again?

In the world of nonelectronic research, we often find ourselves with our favorite sources close at hand, maybe on our desktops or in a nearby bookcase. The Internet equivalents for such security blankets are referred to as bookmarks or favorite places. Good researchers master these tools.

# *PART* **TWO**

## *The Internet Library*

# CHAPTER FOUR

# Accessing the Net

## Online Services

It is just as important to understand how to access the data you need on the Internet as it is to know when and why to use the Net. Indeed, the *how* is critical. You may know that the Net is the cheapest, most current and accurate source, but if you cannot get to the Web site or newsgroup archive, the knowledge is of no use. There are a number of access techniques available, distinguished in terms of cost and, most critically, in terms of ease and immediacy of use.

As a result of the explosive popularity of the World Wide Web, Internet access has been heavily promoted by the commercial online services such as America Online, CompuServe, and the Microsoft Network. These services, which provide access, or *gateways,* to the Net in addition to proprietary (non-Internet) online services, are particularly popular among those who log on from home. They are designed to be easy to use and inexpensive, generally costing just twenty dollars per month. In terms of equipment, all one needs to surf the Web via these services is a personal computer, a modem, and a telephone line. However, given the mass marketing of these largely consumer-oriented online services and the resulting millions of people online, using these services for ongoing, time-sensitive Internet research is not recommended.

In recent years, all of the consumer online services have launched major membership drives that have resulted in massive demand overloads. Simply put, the services passed out more access accounts than their communication lines, modems, and computers could support. All of the services have, at various times, been plagued by severely reduced access speeds as the number of active members has outpaced the ability of the technology to speed data and otherwise support system users. Consequently, class action suits have been filed, charging the services failed to deliver on their service promises. The legal professional, like any serious business researcher, cannot afford to waste time with a research access method that cannot deliver reliably.

The types of access problems one can encounter are many and varied. Users of the consumer-oriented services have experienced prolonged data transfer delays, inexplicable service interruptions resulting in disconnects, and e-mail messages that never arrive. As a result of such poor service levels, the inexperienced Internet user might consider the Internet itself to be an intolerable nuisance. But Net surfers who have experienced more reliable and much faster access recognize the difference between the value of Internet content and the inability of some companies to provide acceptable levels of access to it.

## Internet Service Providers and Local Gateways

Many other books, including Burgess Allison's *The Lawyer's Guide to the Internet* (http://www.abanet.org/lpm/catalog/511-0343.html) and Josh Blackman's *How to Use the Internet for Legal Research* (http://www.internetlawyer.com/book/netlaw.htm), cover how to access the Net in detail. There is no need to repeat that discussion here. However, a brief overview of how access methods affect the researcher may help make your use of the Net for research more effective.

There are three basic Internet access methods. The first, and typically the most costly, method is to set up your own Internet connection, or node. This entails registering a domain name (such as *internetlawyer.com* or *aba.com*) with the Internet Network Information Center (http://rs.internic.net/index2.html), paying the $100 startup fee (which covers registration for two years), and maintaining the computer workstation and software (at about $20,000) that will be connected to a high-speed phone line (for example, a T-1 line, at perhaps $1,000 per month), which in turn is connected to the Internet. Typically, this scenario is an option only for organizations willing to pay the cost and conduct the maintenance required.

At the other end of the spectrum is the second access method, the commercial online service connection (for example, CompuServe or America Online), most typically employed by the less demanding Internet user. Once primarily populated by computer hobbyists, these online services have begun to creep into corporate offices throughout the world, especially in smaller businesses unable to afford a private Internet node.

Given the unpredictability of network connectivity, however, many businesspeople use these services only for e-mail. While the online services may be offering a variety of services in addition to Internet access, including financial information, general reference data, and chat rooms, the technical difficulties plaguing the providers have discouraged many serious business users.

Taking advantage of this trend, a third prong of the Internet access industry, which emerged in the early 1990s, offers a sort of leased access to the Internet. Such Internet service providers (ISPs), including Netcom and UUNet, enable businesses to maintain Internet access without having to maintain a node themselves, and without having to bother with the consumer-orientation of a commercial online service. For organizations too small to maintain their own Internet server computer in-house, yet with a strong need for the sort of Internet access that a commercial service just cannot provide, dialing in (using a computer, modem, and phone line) to an ISP's server is often desirable.

Beyond mere access, however, ISPs also enable businesses to create a Net presence, or node, on the ISPs computer. A law firm can, for example, establish *ourlawfirm.com* on an ISP's server computer and build a Web site there. In this scenario, the labor and maintenance costs involved in setting up a node are shifted to the ISP. Consequently, a smaller or technically limited firm can participate as a Web site provider by hiring an outsourcer to handle the hardware and software, while the firm itself focuses on the content and services offered online. This approach has proved a boon for the entrepreneurial and self-employed, who are able to participate in the Internet services industry alongside major corporations.

Thus the Internet has become the great equalizer, allowing more and more organizations and companies to establish an Internet presence for themselves no matter what their size. This has significant dividends for the individual researcher. It is no longer impossible to contact hard-to-reach organizations. Before the Internet, the only way to reach certain people or companies was by leaving phone messages and hoping they would call back. Now it is possible for a researcher to click over to a competitor's Web site and copy off the pricing schemes for a competing product in complete anonymity, at any time, from any location.

## Internet Structure and Connectivity

The information highway metaphor has some instructive value for the researcher. When using the Net for research purposes, the researcher travels to the sites offered by millions of server computers, all connected via the telephone network. Just because there are tie-ups and traffic jams along the way does not mean one cannot turn around and find alternative routes.

There are many such alternative ways to use the Net, but they cannot be appreciated until the Internet user first understands that the glitches that can inhibit progress are not truly *Internet* problems. More often, they are problems with the service provider, the target source being accessed, or the telecommunications hardware and software on your desk. When you know why you are having trouble reaching the source you need, then you can more easily devise a way around the problem.

For example, many frequently visited Web sites are mirrored, or duplicated, at secondary locations. Very often, mirrored sites are indicated in printed directories and by online search engines like Infoseek and AltaVista. Say you need to draft a licensing agreement relative to digital property, so you search for *licensing digital* on AltaVista (http://altavista.digital.com) and discover that, indeed, Yale University archives the LIBLICENSE discussion list and also provides lots of agreements to choose from. Yale's Licensing Digital Information site is available from two different places, one in the United States (http://www.library.yale.edu/~llicense/index.shtml) and one in France (http://enssibhp.enssib.fr/miroir/liblic/). (See Figure 4.1.) If you try to access the first site and the access speed is very slow, you can try accessing the mirrored site. You would know to do this, however, only if you recognize that mirrored sites exist and that the slow access speed may be due to heavy user traffic in the United States.

One of the more common myths about improving Internet access is that if you buy a faster modem, you will have faster Internet service. This is not necessarily the case, because access speed is subject to many variables, including the age and quality of the telephone lines in your area, whether they are copper or fiber, whether your Internet service provider is having problems, whether you are trying to download lots of graphics, and so on. Essentially, your access speed will be determined by the weakest link in the data transmission chain. Your modem is just one of those links. Misconceptions concerning such issues contribute to user frustration to the point where the Internet is unfairly discounted as a serious research tool. Ongoing developments in various telecommunication technologies, including fiber optics, ISDN (Integrated Services Digital Network), and frame relay, point to a time when all Internet access will be fast all the time. Though such a time is still in the future, that does not mean *you* cannot have fast access all or most of the time.

Net users interested in maximizing the efficient use of their time online can benefit from understanding a bit about the Net's structure. For

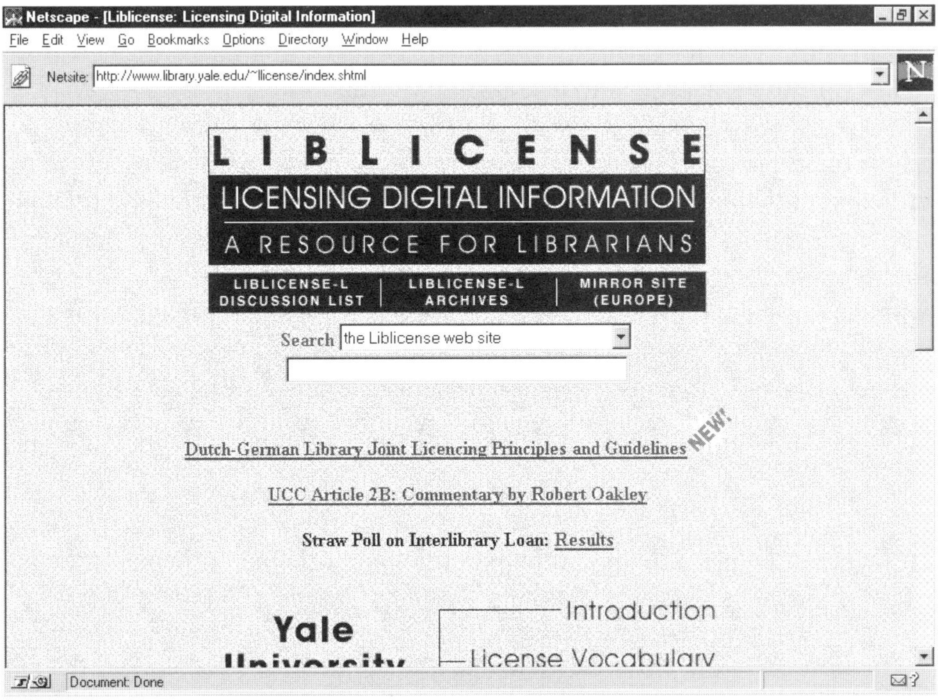


**FIGURE 4.1.** Note the "Mirror Site (Europe)" on this page from the Yale University Library.

example, it is worth knowing that each computer node on the Net is in turn connected to a network hub, which in turn may be connected to another network hub, which is ultimately connected to an Internet backbone. For more insight into the Web's structure and usage statistics, visit InterNic Information Services (http://rs.internic.net/nic-support/) and Cyberatlas (http://www.cyberatlas.com/).

The point is that the Net is a complex of many smaller networks. This network of networks was designed for the U.S. Defense Department such that when failures do occur, network traffic finds a way to reroute itself. The complexity of the network, the extreme amount of data traffic it carries, and the millions of individual computers and telecommunication switches it depends on means that failures do occur. Data traffic is affected by the technical limitations and flaws in our local equipment as well as the gear in place at remote sites we access. We are also subject to the data transfer limitations of the telephone service providers. If we are using an Internet service provider or commercial online service, we are similarly limited by the types of configurations they use. Finally, since using the Internet means communicating via wire and radio waves, our research is affected by the quirks of the environment.

One good thunderstorm can still wreak havoc on any telecommunication activity; wireless laptop Internet access is still a no-go in the Chunnel or on the Concorde; and one too many Net surfers attempting to download the entire Pre-Byzantine Exhibition at the Vatican can bring Internet access for dozens of others to a screeching halt. Again, the critical factor is how we access the Net, not the Internet itself.

Savvy Internet users understand this and take pains to consider factors affecting access before going online. East Coast researchers, for example, may wish to log on to bibliographic search services (AskERIC [http://ericir.syr.edu/], for example, is a bibliographic source in the field of education, psychology, sociology, and information science) as early as possible, before other users begin to heat up the network. This beating-the-rush technique takes on almost mythical proportions within the diehard Net-surfing community. Here are some other techniques that are key to maximizing Net-use efficiency:

- *Schedule Internet activity based on time zones.* For example, East and West Coast users can stagger online time to minimize network congestion; New York researchers can take advantage of the early morning hours, while those in San Francisco might consider using the hours after 2 P.M.
- *Avoid sites during seasonally or temporally sensitive times.* For example, most federal government sites are busiest during the middle of the day and during annual crunch periods such as tax-filing season or election time. You may find it difficult, for example, to reach the National Retail Federation (http://www.nrf.com/) during holiday shopping season.
- *Refrain from downloading or uploading large data files during peak activity hours.*
- *Do not access highly graphical sites with low-performance computers or modems.* Another alternative is to turn off the graphics option in your browser.
- *Do not opt for graphical displays when text-only is sufficient.* If a Web site provides a text-only option, choosing it may speed your research time.

While none of these techniques alone will radically improve your research performance, collectively they illustrate how frequent users of the Net can make the technology work for them rather than against them. If an Internet user keeps such considerations in mind, he or she will be more successful at finding just the information needed in the shortest time possible.

# CHAPTER FIVE

# Navigating the Net

## Web Browsers

While all of the Web browser software (including Netscape Navigator, Microsoft Internet Explorer, and the browsers built into online services like Netcom, America Online [AOL], and CompuServe) perform basically the same functions, they each have their own characteristics. However, the competition between Netscape and Microsoft for browser market share has resulted in such an incredibly rapid evolutionary pace (new versions of Navigator and Explorer are released every six months or so) that it is pointless to discuss these features in any depth. Any such discussion will soon be irrelevant.

It is worth noting, however, the essential browser features that the researcher ought to be familiar with. Any good browser will provide the ability to bookmark favorite Internet sites, easily access those bookmarks, and move backward and forward between Web pages. Another typical browser feature is one common to all graphical user interface software—the ability to cut and paste. Browsers enable you to copy text from Web sites and paste it into software such as word processors. This can be a very handy feature.

Say you are conducting research designed to challenge your opponent's expert witness. If the expert is a physician, you might click over to the American Medical Association's site (http://www.ama-assn.org/) to get the expert's background information. Once you find her address, school attended, and other basics, you might highlight the data with your mouse, copy it using the CTRL-C sequence (holding down the CTRL key and hitting C), bring up your word processor, and paste it (using the CTRL-V keystrokes) onto the dossier page you are building.

Another excellent browser feature is the ability to conduct a text search on any Web page viewable in your browser. Say, for example, you are interested in adding to your law firm's corporate clients. As part of the preparation for your marketing effort, you would like to look into a particular target company's recent legal matters. Assuming your target is a public company, you might start by looking at the relevant portion of the 10-K filing (Part 1, Item C, Legal Proceedings). So, you could click over to EDGAR (**http://www.sec.gov/cgi-bin/srch-edgar**) and pull up the 10-K. Then, if you are using Navigator or Explorer, you could hit CTRL-F to invoke the Find tool. Note that this tool searches only the document that appears in the browser window. It does not search the entire Web the way search engines like AltaVista and Infoseek do. When the Find search window pops up, type LEGAL (uppercase or lowercase letters make no difference), hit return, and you should be taken to the Legal Proceedings section. (See Figure 5.1.)

Browsers are evolving in a couple different directions. Following the general personal computer software trend that began in the 1980s, brows-

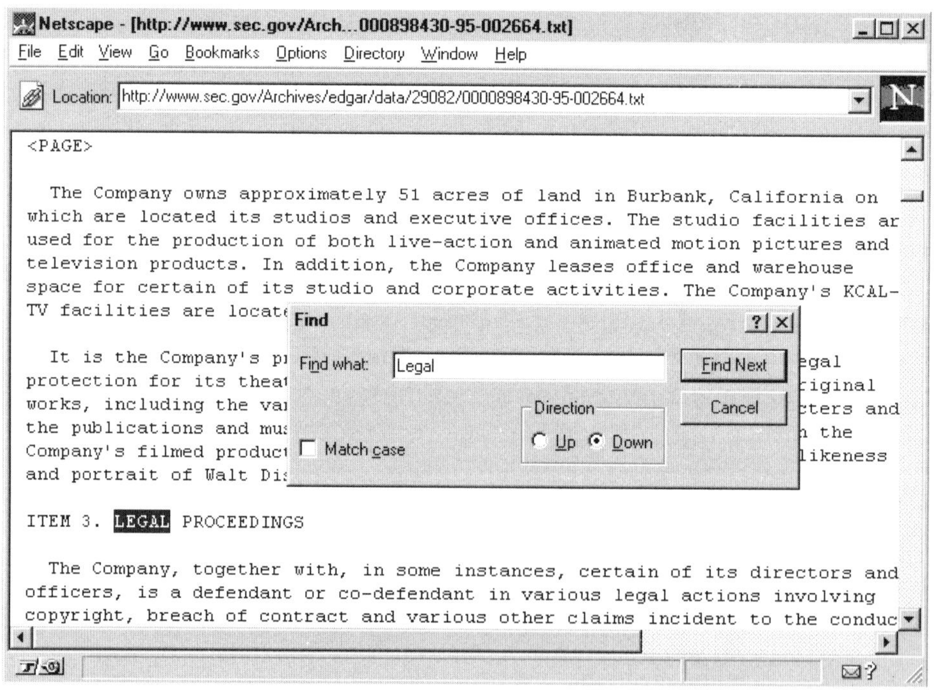


**FIGURE 5.1.** Here is a demonstration that uses the Find search tool to locate the Legal Proceedings section of a Walt Disney Company 10-K from the SEC's EDGAR site.

ers are being subsumed within and combined with other software. For example, a browser can be invoked from within your word-processing program. Features such as e-mail and Web page editing have been incorporated, expanding browser functionality. The expectation is that within a short time, the browser interface—that is, the window through which we view the Internet—will become the primary way we view all personal computing tasks. We will compose and edit documents there, e-mail them to colleagues, access the Internet and our firm's in-house intranet, use spreadsheet software, and so forth, all through a single, consistent window in our computer screens. Such consistency has not yet been achieved across the Internet, though it is getting closer all the time.

Choosing a Web browser boils down to personal preferences. Especially given the Microsoft-Netscape battle for desktop supremacy, the leading browsers are functionally identical. You may have a preference, however, for the way Netscape handles bookmarks, or the screen layout employed by Explorer.

Those without the luxury of an in-house computer support staff must decide for themselves whether to follow the software developers and download the latest browser version. (See Figure 5.2.) This points out one of the few advantages of the commercial online services, particularly America Online, with regard to Web access. Since AOL aims to be easy to use, you do not have to do anything to ensure you are using the latest AOL Web browser. When you log on, AOL will determine whether you have the latest software and, if not, download it for you. The flip side of this is that AOL does not frequently upgrade its Web browser.

Other than this software upgrade feature, AOL and its breed do not bring much to the table when it comes to using the Web. In fact, they can detract from the experience. For example, their proprietary browsers cannot match the sophistication of Navigator and Explorer. (Note that it is possible to use alternative browsers with AOL, though it is not simple. See http://www.lifelines.com/aolhelp.html.) In addition, some of the commercial services, including AOL, restrict your access to the Web. For example, AOL screens out Web sites displaying certain words and graphics. Pornography, for example, is not accessible via America Online's Web connection. Of course, in the workplace one generally does not need access to pornography. However, the screening function is rather imperfect, preventing access to sites that are otherwise inoffensive and, in fact, useful to the business researcher.

AOL and the other commercial online services (CompuServe, Prodigy, and the Microsoft Network) are fine for Internet beginners. Each of these services offers telephone support, relatively easy-to-install software, fixed pricing plans, e-mail, proprietary content, and Internet access. However,

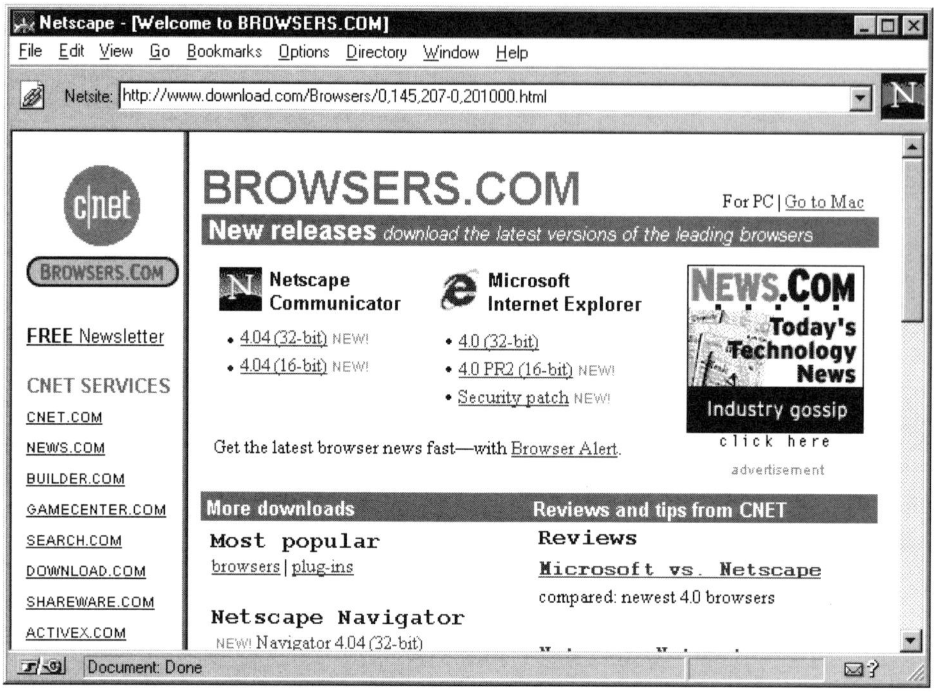




**FIGURE 5.2.** This CNET-owned site enables you to download the latest version of all Web browsers and plug-ins. It also provides links to Internet software articles, and a counter that indicates the number of times each program has been downloaded.

for the experienced business user, a better bet for Internet access is one of the dedicated Internet access providers. National examples (which are convenient if you travel) of ISPs include Netcom and AT&T WorldNet, although there are a total of some four thousand ISPs, most of them serving local regions. (See Figure 5.3.)

## Search Engines

Next to the browsers, the most important Internet software tools are the various Web search engines. Some of the most prominent of these include Yahoo, Lycos, Infoseek, AltaVista, and Excite. While search engines have made finding Web sites far easier, they all fail to provide the key element that a good researcher requires: a consistent, versatile searching methodology or protocol.

All search engines claim to provide Boolean capabilities (the ability to use logical connectors, such as *and, or, within,* and so forth), which they

**FIGURE 5.3.** There is something ironic about looking for an Internet service provider on the Internet, but it is the best place to look. The List is the best-known ISP list, conveniently arranging some four thousand ISPs by area code and country.

do to a limited extent. But none of them offer the level of search sophistication that online researchers have come to expect from sophisticated services like LEXIS and DIALOG. Essentially, standard professional search protocols enable you to pinpoint anything in the database, assuming you are proficient at using the search tool. Internet search engines cannot do that.

One of the frequent complaints concerning search engines is that they return too much irrelevant information in response to search requests. Admittedly, at times when the researcher has no clue what is ultimately sought and needs the search software to essentially make suggestions in the form of varied Web destinations, this search engine flaw is a good thing. But the more common and disappointing experience is to receive two thousand responses to a simple request, which then need to be scanned through, page by page, until a responsive site is found.

To their credit, the search engines generally do a fairly good job of returning something useful in the first few hits. It would be a poor use of time to scroll through two thousand responses. The experienced researcher can sense right away whether the responses are relevant and likely to lead to an appropriate site. If the first few hits are irrelevant, the best thing to do is to reissue a revised search request.

The quality of search results is an important search engine distinction. Such results can also separate the experienced researcher from the novice. A lousy search strategy will be unsuccessful no matter which search software is used, and a precise search string will generate better results with the weakest search tool. The optimal situation is for the researcher to understand the nuances of each engine and to submit focused search requests that take advantage of such nuances. This takes practice, but it is possible. It also requires paying attention to the search engine enhancements that are frequently added.

The best way to learn how each search engine works is to read the Help or Tips pages available at each engine's site. Such instructions demonstrate how the designers recommend using the engine. What the Help pages do not usually tell you is exactly how the engine was built or how the search algorithms weight the search string elements you submit. This is the stuff that truly determines how the engines work and why they pull up some pages instead of others. After reading the Help pages, the next best way to learn how to use search engines effectively is simply to use them. Familiarity leads to expertise. By trying out various engines and using them frequently, you will get a sense of the strengths and weaknesses of each.

If you take the time to read the instructions, your searches will be more accurate. One thing you will find, however, if you study the various engines is that search protocols are different for each engine. Some vary slightly from each other, and some vary a lot. What works well on AltaVista may not work at all on Infoseek. Remembering what search syntax to use at which site can be a challenge.

A good example of this inconsistency is the way search tools rank search results. For example, AltaVista's advanced search provides a ranking box that you can use to influence the order in which results appear. By entering the words *experienced* and *trial* in the ranking field, you could focus a search for a demolition expert. If you do not put anything in the ranking box, results appear in random order, which is less useful. AltaVista's advanced search also enables you to enter date restrictions so that search results are limited to documents last modified during the time frame you specify. This assumes that the modification date information that AltaVista receives from the computer where the found page exists is accurate. Also keep in mind that a modification date does not necessarily imply anything more than a minor modification.

The existing Web search technology is generally unable to handle compound search statements. For example, you cannot (with rare exceptions) nest search queries, such as *heirloom and (antiques and (chicago or new york))*. Very few Web search tools offer truncation (the ability to search for word extensions using a wild-card character, such as an asterisk). For example, if you wanted to search for all words that start with the word *silver*, you could enter *silver**, and the engine would return results including *silverware, silversmith, silverfish,* and so on. In addition, few engines offer sophisticated proximity capabilities (to find concepts or words near each other). Those engines that do offer these features can be limited. For example, AltaVista has a NEAR operator, but it will only find documents containing both specified words or phrases within ten words of each other. If you want the engine to find words or phrases within twelve words of each other, or five, you are out of luck.

While there are syntactical and functional differences among the engines, there are also similarities. For example, if you want to search for a precise word pattern (a full name or phrase), the common practice is to enclose the word pattern in quotation marks. Most of the engines also provide the ability to exclude certain words from your search. Lycos uses the minus (-) command in front of any word that you want to screen out. For example, if you were searching for magazines but wanted to avoid computer magazines, you could use this search phrase when using Lycos: *magazine-computer*. AltaVista excludes terms using the AND NOT connector. For example, if you wanted to find documents containing the word *Mary* but not *lamb*, the proper search phrase using AltaVista is *Mary AND NOT lamb*. On AltaVista's Advanced Search Help page you will find definitions of all the Boolean connectors available.

A study comparing five search engines (AltaVista, Excite, HotBot, Infoseek, and Lycos) for precision was conducted in 1997 (http://www.winona.msus.edu/is-f/library-f/webind2/webind2.htm). The analysis shows that AltaVista, Excite, and Infoseek are the top three services. Lycos was found to perform better on short, unstructured queries, while HotBot performed better on structured queries. Another search engine analysis (http://www.cs.uga.edu/~burson/gis/search.html#HDR0) found Excite to be the most precise Internet search tool. In early 1996, *PC World* rated Lycos the best (http://www.pcworld.com/reprints/lycos.htm). Also in 1996, *PC Magazine* called Excite "the best general-purpose Web search site" (http://www8.zdnet.com/pcmag/iu/srchsite/ec.htm). As with Web browsers, choosing "the best" search engine is a personal decision. The varying characteristics of each search engine argue for learning one or two of them well and sticking with those. See Table 5.1 for an overview of the major search engines.

**TABLE 5.1.** Internet search engine comparison.

| Engine | URL | Indexes | Comments |
|---|---|---|---|
| AltaVista | http://altavista.digital.com | Web, newsgroups | Most sophisticated search engine. Features include NEAR connector, asterisk wildcard, and a Refine feature to narrow your search. Will search in many languages and within date limitations. To get the benefits of these features, you ought to learn to use the advanced features. |
| DejaNews | http://www.dejanews.com/ | Newsgroups, yellow pages | Probably the best newsgroup search engine. Will search by author, subject, date, and newsgroup. |
| Excite | http://www.excite.com/ | Web, newsgroups | Offers subject index and advanced search. Recommends searching for ideas and concepts rather than keywords. Offers a More-Like-This relevancy feature. |
| FindLaw | http://www.findlaw.com | Legal sites on Web, law reviews, Web, legal mailing lists, U.S. government, U.S. Code, U.S. Supreme Court | Premier legal search engine. |
| Galaxy | http://galaxy.einet.net/galaxy.html#SEARCH | Web | This is primarily a directory but also enables searching of gopher and telnet resources. |
| HotBot | http://www.hotbot.com/ | Web, newsgroups | Fast. Allows choice of 10 to 100 hits. Will respond with full or brief description or just URL. |

## Metasearch Engines

Another variety of Internet search tool is the *metasearch engine,* which enables searching several individual search engines at once. These tools are good for searching for very obscure subjects and for searching the most Web space possible. The downside of these tools is that they are generally less precise and accurate. Here are a few metaengines:

- The Internet Sleuth (**http://isleuth.com/**)
- Metacrawler (**http://www.metacrawler.com/**)
- All In One Search (**http://www.albany.net//allinone/all1www.html**)
- Searcher (**http://cpcug.org/user/jlacombe/search.html**)

**TABLE 5.1.** (Continued)

| Engine | URL | Indexes | Comments |
|---|---|---|---|
| Infoseek | http:// www.infoseek.com/ | Web, newsgroups, news wires, company profiles, e-mail addresses, news | Fast. Offers subject index and advanced search. |
| Lycos | http://lycos.com/ | Web, sounds, pictures, top 5%, personal home pages, UPS tracking | Offers subject index. |
| Magellan | http:// www.mckinley.com/ | Web, reviewed sites | Offers advanced search. Searches by concept. |
| Open Text Index | http:// index.opentext.net/ | Web, newsgroups, e-mail, current events | Powersearch option enables limiting searching within summary, heading, or URL. Also offers BUT NOT operator to avoid terms. |
| Reference.Com | http:// www.reference.com/ | Newsgroups, mailing lists | Offers unique feature: will alert you when anyone posts a message to a newsgroup that mentions a word or phrase you select. |
| Search.Com | http://search.com/ | Web | This is a CNET service. Offers subject index. |
| WebCrawler | http:// www.webcrawler.com/ | Web | Offers subject index. |
| Yahoo | http://www.yahoo.com/ | Yahoo, newsgroups, e-mail addresses | Extensive, human-created subject index. Allows searching by time period (1 day to 3 years) and limiting hits from 10 to 100. |

## Search Engine Tips

Here are a few key tips for using search engines effectively:

- *Try using both simple and advanced search options.* Very often, you will get different results using each approach. Also try using more than one search engine per search.
- *Keep in mind that the order in which you type keywords makes no difference in search results.*
- *If you plan to rerun a search, consider bookmarking the search results page.* Some engines, including AltaVista, will rerun the search when you return to the page.

- *Remember that no search engine can actually search the entire Web,* no matter what the propaganda says. Among the places no public search engine can catalog are sites requiring passwords, graphics or portable document format (PDF) files (see Figure 5.4), and the content of sites that can be viewed only by searching a database at the site.
- *Consider getting software to help manage your bookmarks.* MeltingPoint (http://www.docuwork.com/) is such a product designed for legal professionals. *PC Magazine* reviewed nine Internet organizers in May 1996 (http://www8.zdnet.com/pcmag/issues/1509/pcmg0099.htm).

## ADDITIONAL SEARCH ENGINE RESOURCES

### Choosing a Web Search Service

http://www.infotoday.com/searcher/may/story3.htm

**FIGURE 5.4.** Portable document format (PDF) files can be viewed or printed on most computers and have the benefit of appearing *exactly* identical, no matter where they are viewed or printed. This is particularly useful in the case of government forms (IRS forms, for example). You will need a PDF viewer to view and print such documents. The freely available Adobe Acrobat is the best-known PDF viewer.

Search Engine Comparison Chart

http://www.kcpl.lib.mo.us/search/chart.htm

Search Engine Watch

http://searchenginewatch.com/

## Subject Guides and Directories

Search sites on the Internet come in two flavors. First, there are the search engines or indexes, which use programs that scan the Web and index the contents of Web pages into massive databases through which you can search. Second, there are subject guides or directories, which are lists of Web sites organized into subject categories through which you can also search. Search indexes are created by computers, while subject guides are created by humans. Subject guides are generally less voluminous than the databases created by search engines, and, sometimes, using a subject guide is simply an easier way to find what you need. A guide of recommended sites compiled by a human editor can be much more helpful than the results a computer algorithm displays.

Some search sites (AltaVista, Open Text Index, and HotBot) are pure Web indexes. Some (Excite, Infoseek, Lycos, and WebCrawler) combine indexes and directories. Finally, some (FindLaw, Galaxy, Magellan, and Yahoo) are primarily subject guides. (See Figure 5.5.)

## Newsgroups

The ease of conducting primary research on the Internet is one of the most unique features of the technology. Before the Net, such a cheap, ubiquitous, and multidisciplinary vehicle for networking with the international community simply did not exist. Internet newsgroups are the closest things to the original computerized community: the electronic bulletin board systems (BBSs). The critical distinction between BBSs (which are still popular to a limited degree) and Internet newsgroups is that BBSs generally exist on stand-alone computers. They are reached by dialing in, via modem. BBS conversations generally take place on that one computer. By contrast, Internet newsgroup conversations essentially take place on millions of computers. The same conversations can be viewed and participated in by anyone with newsgroup access (and anyone with

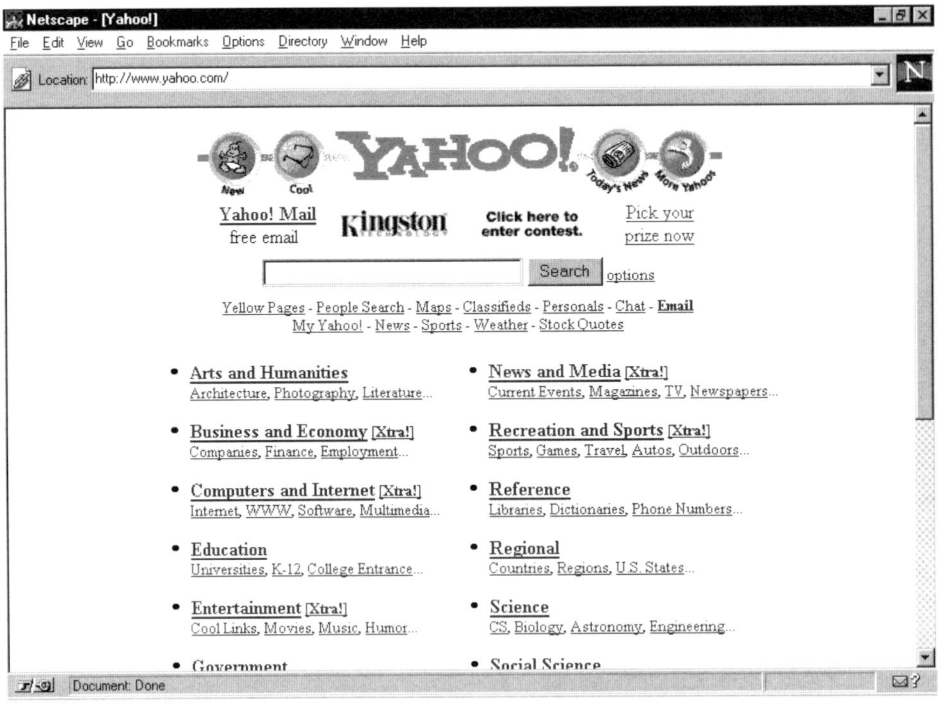




**FIGURE 5.5.** Yahoo is the most popular subject guide, providing a wide variety of topics to choose from, which in turn provide lists of topical Web sites.

Web access has newsgroup access). Unlike BBSs, therefore, newsgroups offer a much more robust forum for communal information sharing.

What this means for the Internet researcher is that newsgroups can be jumped into and out of while carrying out research elsewhere on the Net. This seamlessness makes it possible for the researcher to post questions, observations, or problems for other newsgroup participants to respond to, without having to disconnect his or her phone connection from one electronic research service and then dial into another, as is the case with BBSs. This ability to be in two places at the same time is extremely valuable to the researcher, especially when operating under time constraints.

When a Net researcher stumbles upon something baffling, it is quite easy to select a newsgroup by topic and post a query for review by others who frequent that group. In this way, the Net virtually does your work for you. You can check back in the newsgroup periodically, within hours or weeks, to see whether anyone has responded to your query. (See Figure 5.6.)

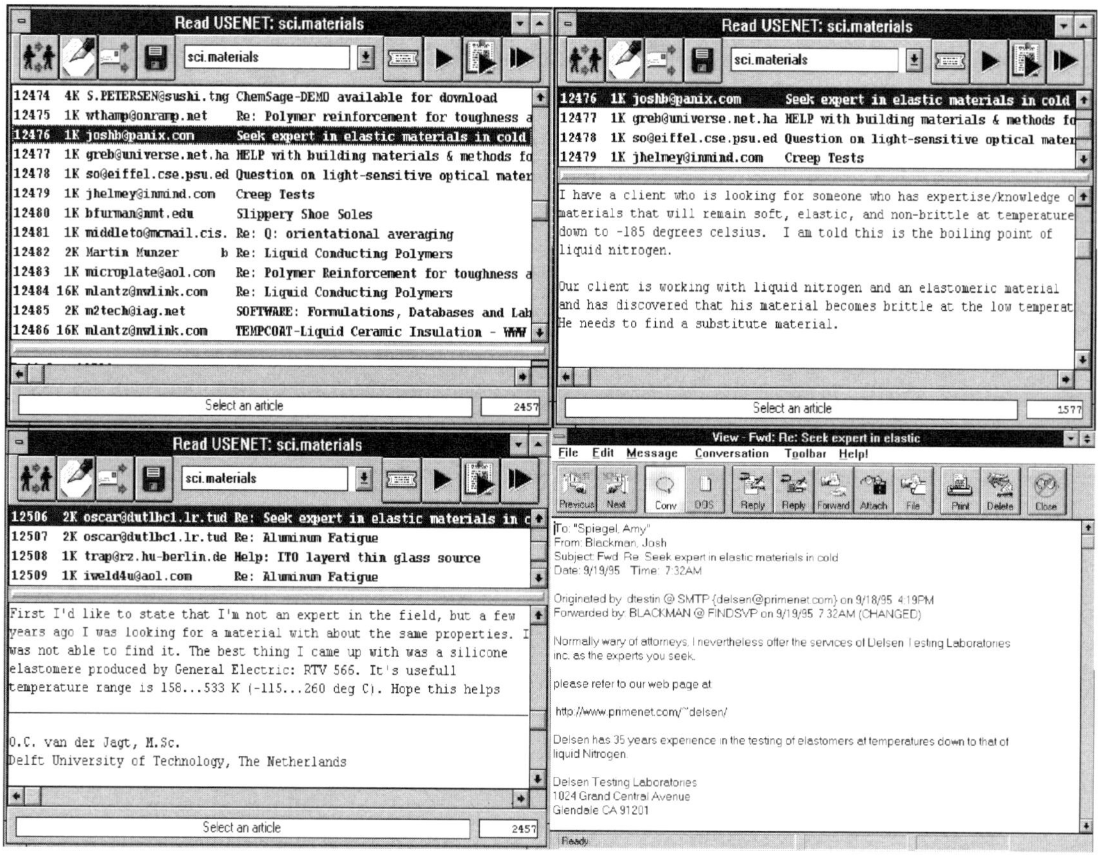

**FIGURE 5.6.** These four screens illustrate how newsgroups can answer tough questions. The screen at upper left highlights the message posted in the group "sci.materials" (focuses on materials science questions). At upper right is the question posed. At bottom left is a response from an individual at Delft University in the Netherlands. At bottom right is another response, which was copied from the newsgroup and forwarded via e-mail.

## Accessing Newsgroups

The easiest way to read newsgroup articles on a particular subject is via DejaNews (http://www.dejanews.com). This site provides an intuitive search-engine-type window on newsgroup content. You can post messages to groups and search groups by subject, using keywords. You can also use DejaNews to find all the messages posted by a particular individual. This is rather useful in situations where you are investigating an expert who may be testifying for the opposition. DejaNews also enables browsing through all the messages in a particular newsgroup and selecting newsgroups based on broad categories.

Other search engines, including AltaVista, Yahoo, and Infoseek, also enable searching through newsgroups. FindLaw offers a database of legally oriented groups. Liszt features a newsgroup directory (**http://www.liszt.com/news/**). Another way to access newsgroups is by acquiring newsreader software, which generally is provided by your Internet service provider. Such software can be loaded into your Web browser, so that you can view newsgroups via the browser.

Newsgroups are frequently confused with listservs by new Internet users. They are similar in that they both comprise discussion forums on thousands of topics. The primary difference is that newsgroups reside in a database form, such that you need to go to the newsgroup database to view messages. Listservs (also known as mailing lists), by contrast, are e-mailed directly to your e-mail box. You do not need to go anywhere to read listserv messages; they come to you. To further complicate the issue, some listservs are archived, in which case they too exist in a database form that you can go to.

## *Listservs*

The most commonly misspelled Internet research source, listservs derive their names from the servers that drive them. In the computer naming protocols of days gone by, when file names were required to be a fixed length of eight characters (thus, *listserv*), computer network servers were the masters of the mailing lists that resided on them. These Internet mailing lists are among the oldest, most popular, and most useful features of the Net.

As the name implies, listservs provide a mechanism by which Internet users across the world, with some common interests, can communicate with each other by sending mass mailings amongst themselves. For example, professional technical writers on the Internet can subscribe to the Technical Writers List, TECH-WRL. With a single post, or message, a Net user (who does not necessarily have to be a subscriber or member of the list) can distribute a message to all Net members of the list. Note, however, that some listservs are moderated, meaning every message posted is reviewed by an editor before it is released to list subscribers.

Listservs are often a mixed blessing to Internet users because many subscribers are unaware of the high volume of messages that some listservs generate. Excessive e-mail traffic generated by listserv subscriptions at the workplace have frequently raised the ire of network administrators, and many listserv managers have begun offering listserv digests as alternatives to individually transmitted listserv messages.

There is far more anonymity for the message poster in a newsgroup than in a listserv, and this anonymity can be beneficial when conducting confidential research. Listserv communications move through subscribers' e-mail boxes and are therefore preferable over newsgroup messages when conducting survey research or polling activities that require targeted audiences of particular qualifications.

An added advantage of listservs is that they constitute the one and only Internet function that does not require any type of Internet access to use them. All that is necessary is an e-mail address. Since listservs do not physically reside within the Internet itself, the Net is used only to transmit these messages, not to view them.

## ADDITIONAL LISTSERV RESOURCES

Tilenet—Lists of listservs.

http://tile.net/listserv/

Additional Info on Legal Lists

http://www.regent.edu/lawlib/lists/list-law.html

Easy Subscription to Legal Listservs

http://www.lawguru.com/subscribe/listtool.html

LawLists—The most comprehensive list of legal listservs.

http://www.lib.uchicago.edu/~llou/lawlists/info.html

## BASIC RESOURCES FOR AN INTERNET LIBRARY

### Area Codes

Search.com

http://www.555-1212.com/aclookup.html

### Atlas

U.S. Street Maps

http://www.mapblast.com/

MapQuest—Interactive atlas.

http://www.mapquest.com/

World Maps

http://www.lib.utexas.edu/Libs/PCL/Map_collection/Map_collection.html

### Case Citation Guide

*Bluebook*

http://www.law.cornell.edu/citation/citation.table.html

### Dictionary

Merriam-Webster

http://www.m-w.com/netdict.htm

One Look—Links to dozens of specialized dictionaries, including pronunciation, slang, acronym, medical, sports, science, religion, and technology-related dictionaries.

http://www.onelook.com/

### Legal Dictionaries

*Black's Corporation Law Dictionary*

http://www.alaska.net/~winter/black_law_dictionary.html

"Plain Language" Legal Dictionary

http://www.wwlia.org/diction.htm

'Lectric Law Library Legal Terms

http://www.lectlaw.com/d-a.htm

European Law Dictionary—Eurodicautom is a translator to and from Danish, Dutch, English, French, German, Italian, Portuguese, Spanish, Swedish, and Finnish. Search for terms or abbreviations and limit by subjects, including customs, economics, employment, environment, finance, insurance, law, taxation, telecom, and trade.

http://www2.echo.lu/edic/

## Library Catalogs

Yahoo's Library Collection

http://www.yahoo.com/Reference/Libraries/

Law Library Links

http://law.house.gov/114.htm

## Phone Directory—Toll Free

AT&T

http://www.tollfree.att.net/dir800/

## Thesaurus

Merriam-Webster

http://www.m-w.com/mw/theslimt.htm

## Zip Codes

U.S. Postal Service

http://www.usps.gov/ncsc/lookups/lookup_zip+4.html

# *PART* **THREE**

## *Putting It into Practice*

# CHAPTER SIX

# How to Get News on the Net

A NUMBER OF INTERVIEWS WERE CONDUCTED in the course of writing this book. When we asked lawyers what they were using the Internet for, one of the most common answers involved keeping up-to-date and staying aware of events in the law, in industry, and in the world that pertain to client matters and to developing law firm business. The Internet has added yet another source to our already media-rich environment. But more than simply another periodical, database, or cable TV channel, the Internet has several unique features that recommend its addition to our arsenal of worthy sources.

The interactive nature of the Net is probably its most unique aspect. Online mailing lists and newsgroups enable similarly minded individuals to conveniently meet and correspond. Insurance defense counsel, for example, who need to know what medical professionals have to say about the latest HMO trends can review the conversational archive or actually make contact with the people who are driving the trends or are affected by them, or both. New-media lawyers who need to keep up with the rapidly evolving industry can read online newsletters and do quick scans of online news services to see who has merged with whom, or what new technology is taking off.

The immediacy of the Internet and the way it facilitates information distribution hold strong appeal to lawyers and others who can gain competitive advantage by acting quickly on fresh information. Just as news radio and CNN offer singular facets of immediate news (the radio is perfect for listening while driving; CNN can display helicopter video while events are unfolding), so the Internet offers immediate international distribution of news to desktops set up with push software (for example, Pointcast [http://www.pointcast.com/] or the Yahoo News Ticker [http://www.my.yahoo.com/ticker.html]). Internet mailing lists can immediately distribute messages that may be of interest only to, for example, corporate lawyers, while the major media might not even carry such limited-interest, yet vital, information. If a government agency releases a new finding or rule or news release online, the Internet enables anyone and everyone who needs access to the document to get it at virtually the same time. There is no need to wait for the mail or the fax or the commercial database to provide access.

Finally, the ability to retrieve free information at will from a wide range of publishers, including established newspapers, upstart news services, and individuals who are simply speaking their minds (informed and otherwise) in discussion forums, is another Internet feature that cannot be ignored. Over a very brief period of time, the Internet has established itself as the virtual library that is easy to use, inexpensive, and, for many of us, essential.

## ■ SUCCESS STORY: TED CLAYPOOLE

"Every morning," says lawyer Ted Claypoole,

> I get involved in several listserv groups and online newsletters that allow me to keep up-to-date with what is going on in the law. Therefore, I effectively use the Internet for research every day.
>
> I have one client named ACE Software. It is obviously a very common name and one that you probably could not register if you set out to do it now. Anything relating to software is probably taken at this point. I occasionally check [the Net] on behalf of ACE to see how many new ACE Softwares have popped up, because at some point we are going to be prosecuting that trademark.
>
> I am a business lawyer in Columbus, Ohio. Among other things, I have used the Internet to research names for client businesses and their products. For example, a client named Fifth Wave Solutions was interested in finding interesting names to advertise its line of services. To help this effort, I researched the names of the best surfing beaches in the world through a series of surfing sites, including sites in Australia, Brazil, South Africa, Hawaii, and California. Fifth Wave used the research in its marketing. When a lawyer represents a small business, he is frequently more business consultant than legal consultant.
>
> It was brainstorming. They ended up using Malibu Standard. [Some of the others] were the Bell Beach Basic, which was a major surfing beach in Victoria in southern Australia. One of the products was named

Ooba Tuba, because they liked the name. [That's] a beach outside of São Paulo, Brazil, that is supposed to be very good.

I do that [sort of Internet brainstorming] fairly regularly. I consider myself a business consultant as well as a lawyer. Many of my clients are small to medium-size businesses. Others are start-ups that are just beginning to feel their way in the business world, and they don't have time or money to hire a lot of consultants.

I am a young lawyer, so I try to build my practice through relationships. Part of that is taking an active interest in all the business aspects of my clients' businesses. If I can help them be successful so they are a large company ten years from now, and I am still their lawyer, then we have grown together. So on aspects like surfing, I try to help my clients figure out what kinds of names they want to use—figure out what they should be looking at. Some of that is trademarks, and some of that is just pure basic brainstorming. ■

## News on the Net

There are many news sources on the Internet. Some are World Wide Web versions of well-known media sources such as CNN, *USA Today,* the *Wall Street Journal,* and so forth (see Figure 6.1). Often the same media source that charges a fee for its information on a commercial database (such as LEXIS or Knight-Ridder's DIALOG service) will provide content on the Net for free.

However, that does not necessarily imply that the content on the Net *duplicates* what is found on the commercial sources or what was originally disseminated by the media source. There are frequently differences between Internet versions and what is provided by the same media source elsewhere. For example, there may be a limit to the number of articles displayed on the Net from each edition of a periodical. Or only headlines may be provided, or the news may be summarized.

This is not to say Net news sites do not have value. On the contrary, at the CNN site and several others, you get up-to-the-minute news. Net sites provide you with the unique ability to choose the topics you want to see when you want to see them. In addition, many sites provide archives that can be searched at your leisure.

Here are two examples of Internet news sources that provide true value not available in a similar form (if at all) elsewhere: The *Associated Press Reports* site (http://www.trib.com/NEWS/APwire.html) includes regional reports available only erratically from commercial databases. PRNewswire's Company News On Call pages (http://www.prnewswire.com/) provide

**FIGURE 6.1.** The *Boston Globe* provides free searching of an archive that dates back fifteen years (staff-written stories only). Charges apply ($1.50 per article) for full-text retrieval. The *Globe* site also enables searching of several dozen other U.S. newspapers.

free (versus for-a-fee) access to hundreds of public and private company press releases.

Some news sources are exclusive to the Internet. Whenever a big news story happens, whether it is floods in the Midwest or a war in a developing country, Web pages are set up just to give people a way to exchange information and find ways to help victims. This seems to happen spontaneously. Such is the nature of the Net, the global publishing forum available to everyone.

This trend became very evident during the Oklahoma City bombing and the O.J. Simpson trial. Web sites focusing on these events made it possible to see photos, watch videos, and read news stories and trial transcripts before such materials were available in the press or on television. As we become more accustomed to using the Internet as a news source, and as the Net becomes more commonly available, the immediacy of the Net—the ability to instantly access all the relevant visual and audio elements of an event—will increasingly draw us to the Internet as a news source. When the next big news event occurs, give it a try. Turn on your modem, tune in your favorite search engine, and type out the keyword that best describes the event.

## Discussion Groups

Electronic discussion groups, both newsgroups and mailing lists, are excellent sources for subject-specific news. Such discussion groups track the latest news on a topic and actually enable you to monitor things as they happen. This feature is due to the fact that many members of discussion groups are industry researchers. Newsgroups and listservs do not function merely as news sources for these people. Researchers use discussion groups to exchange ideas and share information about research while it is in progress.

A notable example of this occurred within an AIDS discussion group. Research breakthroughs were made following months of Internet message exchanges among top researchers. Just as with breaking news, some scientific research is being announced on the Internet before making it to scientific journals or traditional news media.

The Internet's ability to deliver information directly from those making news cannot be underestimated. If you need to know as soon as news happens, the Internet is increasingly where you must be. If you need the earliest news about the Bosnian Peace Agreement, you need to join the Bosnet or the Slovak listserv. The messages posted in the newsgroup soc.culture.brazil give you a bird's-eye view of a protest in that country. Likewise, the discussions in the alt.politics groups will make you aware of the latest government issue nuances.

In the Internet's early days (circa 1993), it was not all that easy to sort through discussion groups to find the best groups to monitor or to find discussions on particular subjects. That is no longer the case. A number of newsgroup search engines are now available, including DejaNews, AltaVista, Yahoo, and Infoseek.

Experienced researchers always bring a healthy dose of skepticism to their sources. You should do the same with sources on the Internet. There is no assurance that the information you read in newsgroups is accurate. For that matter, even major news organizations make mistakes. No matter what sources you use, it is always a good idea (though not always possible), if you plan to depend on the information you find, to get independent verification from at least two other sources.

## ■ SUCCESS STORY: JONATHAN EZOR

Jonathan Ezor is an associate with Davis & Gilbert in New York City. He practices new-media law and uses the Internet for legal research several times per day:

> Primarily, what I use [the Net] for is current information about the new-media industry. Business research, really. What are people doing? What software is out there? What tricks are people learning? Who's doing deals with whom? My daily reads include CNET's news section, ZDNet, I/World, various other places like Java World, and the World Wide Web Artists Consortium mailing list is a daily read for me. That comes in via e-mail. Beyond that, I may see an interesting article in Ad Age or the *New York Times* or the *Wall Street Journal* Interactive Edition. I will look at anything available that may be relevant. But CNET (http://www.cnet.com/) is always the first place I turn.
>
> The reason we can be in this breakthrough [area of law] is that we keep up. But it is not merely traditional lawyering. A lot of what we do is business advising. The reason we can do it is because we know where the business is right now. We know what the trends are because we are following them. In fact, we are helping to make them. We know who's doing what. I also do a lot of networking electronically. I have been quoted in a number of publications and never met the reporters or even spoken to them. All of that has led to the marketing side of our competitive advantage. In addition, the information we get on a daily basis is so current that it is the substantive side of our competitive advantage.
>
> If there were no Internet, there wouldn't be what I do. But in terms of access, I know people who are trying to do this sort of work without being [online, but they] just don't get it. It has no reflection on them or their intelligence. It is simply an issue of if you're not a regular user, then you don't understand what regular users need. If you don't know the software, then you don't know the ins and outs of it. It is just so much easier to do this job in the particular area that I am working in having not only a connection, but a high-speed connection. This is a competitive advantage, particularly for a smaller firm that may not be able to bill its clients for LEXIS and the various document services. ■

## NET NEWS RESOURCES

### Newspapers

*Boston Globe*

http://www.boston.com/globe/

*Chicago Tribune*

http://www.chicago.tribune.com/

*Los Angeles Times*

http://www.latimes.com/

*New York Times*

http://www.nytimes.com/

*USA Today*

http://www.usatoday.com/

*Wall Street Research Net*

http://www.wsrn.com:80/home/news.html

*Washington Post*

http://www.washingtonpost.com/

**News Directories**

Editor & Publisher Directory of Online Newspapers

http://www.mediainfo.com/ephome/npaper/nphtm/online.htm

International Press

http://emporium.turnpike.net/~walk/hometown/globe.htm

Internet Sleuth—Searches several news databases.

http://isleuth.com/

Newslink to Online Newspapers, Magazines, & Radio/TV

http://www.newslink.org/menu.html

Total News

http://totalnews.com/

Ultimate Collection of News Links—Contains more than six thousand links.

http://pppp.net/links/news/NA.html

### Radio and TV

ABC News

http://www.abnews.com/

CNN Home Page

http://www.cnn.com/

MSNBC

http://www.msnbc.com/news/default.asp

National Public Radio

http://www.npr.org

WCBS New York News Headlines

http://newsradio88.com/welcome.html

### News Services

NewsPage

http://www.newspage.com/

PR Newswire

http://www.prnewswire.com/

Wire Services Collection

http://www.trib.com/NEWS/APwire.html

## Books and Periodicals

In the business researcher's vernacular, books and periodicals are secondary sources. They are often excellent sources when you need to get smart quickly on all sorts of subjects. Periodicals are particularly useful with regard to current events. The Internet offers several ways to find books and periodicals.

In the case of books, the best the Net will generally do is let you know that a book by a particular author, with a particular title, or concerning a particular subject exists. The Net may also enable you to order the book online. In rare circumstances you can even read a book online for free. This is particularly true for classic literature.

If you are simply trying to find out whether books exist on a topic, you might try one of the many library catalogs online. It is generally a good idea to start off using the broadest catalogs available, such as those at the Library of Congress, the New York Public Library, or the U.S. Copyright Office (although the copyright records on the Net date only from 1978). If you are looking for new books, try one of the catalogs available from retailers like Amazon or Barnes and Noble. All of these options will also enable you to search for titles and authors. If you are looking for books you can read online, consult the On-Line Books Page.

In the case of periodicals, if you do not know the periodical you need, an article abstract search is generally a good start. One of the most groundbreaking products in the realm of electronic information is the UnCover service provided by Knight-Ridder Information (see Figure 6.2).

**FIGURE 6.2.** The Uncover service indexes over eight million articles and provides summaries for each. Use it free (you'll need to create a profile online) to find articles on a broad range of subjects and works by particular authors. In addition, you can choose to have articles faxed directly to you (for a fee).

UnCover demonstrates the wide variety of periodicals available on the Web (it indexes some seventeen thousand periodicals and 8 million articles that have appeared since 1988). Topics of the periodicals included are multidisciplinary, ranging from agriculture to telecommunications.

UnCover is primarily a fee-based article delivery service, although there is no charge to search the database to find whether articles exist. The service is very timely, listing periodicals when they are published (some three thousand new citations are added each day). UnCover began as a way to automate a procedure that had been in place in many libraries and information centers for many years—the automatic routing of tables of contents of major publications, without their covers.

If a general topic-abstracting service is not focused enough, you might wish to consider a more narrow abstracting service, such as Medline, which focuses on medical journals. If you are looking for Web links to newspapers, magazines, journals, or newsletters, consult one of the many excellent catalogs online, including the Electronic Newstand, E•journal, the Association of Research Libraries Directory of Electronic Publications, or the Bulletin Board for Libraries. There are some periodicals completely available on the Net, but they are rare. More commonly, publications post portions of their printed versions on the Net. In many cases, the material free online will provide what you need.

Keep in mind that books and periodicals on the Net are only a portion of your online research sources. In addition to consulting a library catalog or an abstract directory, you also ought to enter your search phrase into one of the search engines to see what other sources are available. By getting familiar with the best sources for your particular needs, you will quickly be able to determine where to go to assemble a bibliography of materials pertinent to the matter at hand.

## BOOK CATALOGS

Out-of-Print Books

http://www.reedref.com/bowker

BookWire (various resources)

http://www.bookwire.com/

Harvard University Library

http://hplus.harvard.edu/

Library of Congress

http://lcweb.loc.gov/

New Books

http://www.amazon.com

http://www.barnesandnoble.com/

The New York Public Library

http://www.nypl.org/

The On-Line Books Page

http://www.cs.cmu.edu/books.html

U.S. Copyright Records (from 1978)

http://lcweb.loc.gov/copyright/rb.html

## PERIODICAL DIRECTORIES

Association of Research Libraries Directory of Electronic Publications

http://www.gold.ac.uk/history/hyperjournal/arl.htm

Bulletin Board for Libraries

http://bubl.ac.uk/link/

dnet—Directory database.

http://www.d-net.com/

E•journal

http://www.edoc.com/ejournal/

Electronic Newstand

http://www.enews.com/

MediaFinder—Includes sixty-two hundred directories listing ninety thousand periodicals (see Figure 6.3).

http://www.mediafinder.com/getlist.htm

Medline—Medical journal abstracts.

http://www.nlm.nih.gov/

TimeWarner magazines

http://pathfinder.com/

UnCover

http://uncweb.carl.org/

**FIGURE 6.3.** MediaFinder provides free access to some sixty-two hundred directories listing ninety thousand periodicals. It is intended to make it easy to request subscriptions and advertising and list rental rates, but it also can alert researchers to the very existence of and contact information for particular magazines, catalogs, newsletters, and newspapers.

# CHAPTER SEVEN

# How to Find Experts on the Net

## Research Techniques

There are plenty of low-tech ways to find experts, whether you need them for testimony or consulting purposes. You can telephone one of the numerous brokerages, not unlike Hollywood talent agencies, that represent experts. These companies can pump résumés and curricula vitae (CVs) through your fax machine to satisfy every esoteric expert need you can think of. They also often charge fees in advance of providing any expertise. You will find scads of ads for these companies as well as for individual experts in the back pages of most legal periodicals, especially those targeted at trial attorneys. Usually, these companies charge a representation fee in addition to the fee you will pay to the expert.

Using the Internet, however, you can find experts faster, and usually cheaper. There are Web sites and discussion forums that specialize in providing access to experts. (See Figure 7.1.) Many experts are even establishing their own Internet sites. You can scan these sources or use the e-mail addresses you will find at many Web sites to directly correspond with appropriate experts. Many of the Web sites that list experts have accepted fees for doing so. The opportunity to use the sites to learn what experts are available and to use the discussion forums to communicate directly with a wide range of experts and colleagues adds value and control to the search process, value and control not available by merely calling an expert broker.

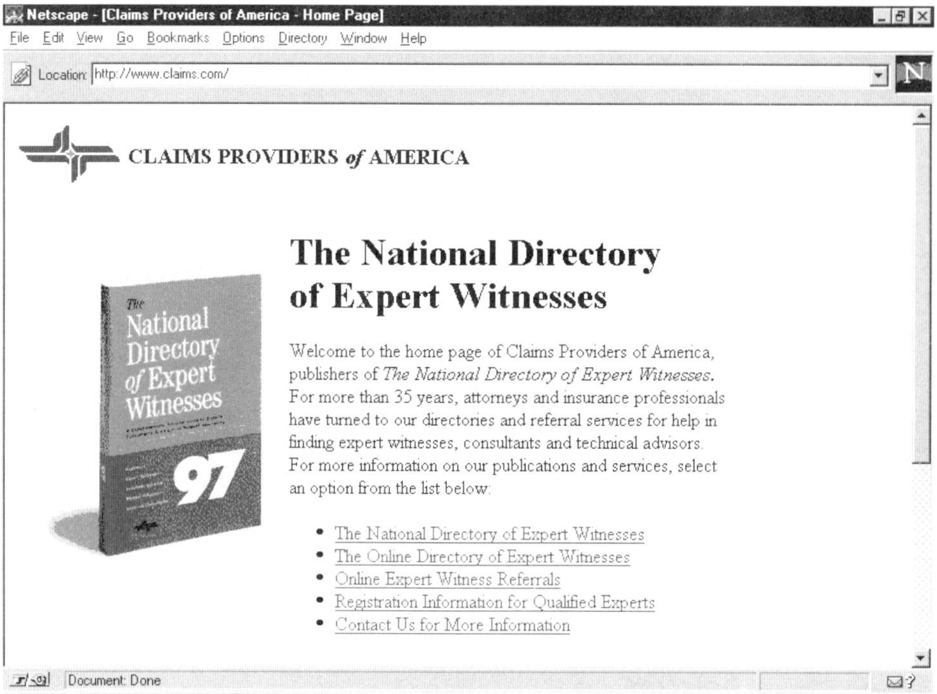


**FIGURE 7.1.** The National Directory of Expert Witnesses is available as a book and as a freely searchable Internet database. It includes an extensive expert directory and is designed specifically for use by law firms and insurance professionals.

The process of locating an expert, however, requires much more than merely finding a name in a directory. The information concerning experts you will find online is just a starting point. It is very important that you conduct a direct interview with any candidates you select, whether by phone, e-mail, or face-to-face. It is also essential to verify the credentials of any expert you consider hiring. (See Figure 7.2.)

In addition to using the specialized expert Web sites, there are many creative ways to find experts. One is to search for articles relevant to the subject in which you seek expertise. For example, if you need a medical expert, consider searching the Medline abstract database (http://www.nlm.nih.gov/). (You will find a list of other periodical directories in "How to Get News on the Net," Chapter 6 of this book.) Another technique is to take advantage of the association community. Every discipline you can imagine, from aardvarks through ZZ Top, has an association that can probably name an expert you can talk to. Many associations publish directories of members, issue publications, and are available to answer questions on the telephone. (You will find a list of association resources in

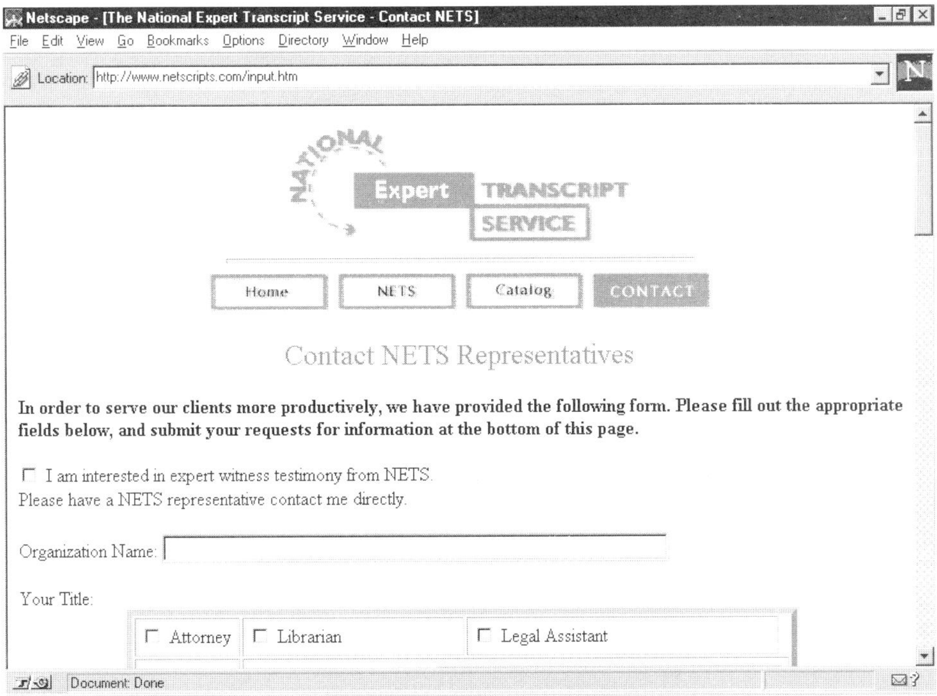


**FIGURE 7.2.** It is important to verify expert credentials. One way to do that is to review transcripts of expert testimony. The Net provides links to several companies that retrieve transcripts, including the National Expert Transcript Service.

"How to Research Companies on the Net," Chapter 9 of this book.) Finally, the government is chock full of experts in all sorts of areas. As with most research, it takes time to cut through the layers of government to find the person who can answer your questions, but if you persevere, you are likely to be rewarded with someone who understands exactly what you are talking about. A good starting place for government agency Web sites (which often include personnel directories) is FindLaw (http://www.findlaw.com).

## ■ SUCCESS STORY: BEN WRIGHT

Ben Wright (Ben_Wright@compuserve.com) is a lawyer in Dallas, Texas, and an expert on digital signatures and electronic contracts. He relates the following episode:

> Julian Ding needed to find an electronic commerce expert—fast. Julian is a partner in Zaid Ibrahim & Company, a larger law firm in Malaysia, a developing country determined to leapfrog itself into leadership on the information highway. The Malaysian parliament was in the process of

adopting digital signature legislation, and Julian's firm wanted to convene a public seminar to examine the topic. To add the requisite cachet, the firm invited the minister of energy, telecommunications, and post to open the seminar.

Unfortunately, the minister confirmed the invitation rather late due to his busy schedule. That left Julian in a bind. He was forced to organize the seminar in thirty days, and he needed to find, among other experts, a foreign lawyer having special experience with digital signatures. So, he turned to Yahoo (**http://www.yahoo.com**) and searched *digital signature,* which yielded the Web page for my book *The Law of Electronic Commerce* (**http://infohaus.com/access/by-seller/Benjamin_Wright**). I obviously knew the skinny on digital signatures because my Web site contains several articles about it. Julian dashed off an e-mail invitation to me, and we soon negotiated an arrangement for me to be present at the event. ■

## Reliability and Relevance of Experts

Harold J. Bursztajn, M.D., is an associate clinical professor of psychiatry at Harvard Medical School. He also has broad courtroom experience as an expert witness in civil and criminal litigation. In his forensic practice, he has consulted to plaintiff and defense counsel and to state and federal agencies as an expert in medical-legal decision making and forensic psychiatry.

Dr. Bursztajn's Web site (**http://www.forensic-psych.com**) focuses on the nexus of forensic psychiatry, medicine, and the law. He offers the following insights regarding using the Net to find medical experts:

> With its emphasis on judicial discretion and the judge as "gatekeeper" for admitting expert testimony, *Daubert v. Merrel Dow Pharmaceuticals, Inc.* 113 S. Ct. 2786 (1993), has been slowly but steadily transforming how attorneys seek experts. With the increasing likelihood that an expert's testimony will face judicial scrutiny, the reliability and relevance of an expert's analysis and evaluation needs to be established long before trial; ideally prior to retaining an expert. While the specific guidelines enumerated by the Supreme Court for scientific testimony are most often used to evaluate the quantitative sciences, the more general criteria of reliability and relevance are increasingly used by judges to evaluate the admissibility of applied science–based expert medical opinion.
>
> One of my most common forensic consultations is to evaluate another "expert's" opinion. When I analyze it as unreliable or irrelevant on medical decision analytic grounds, the attorney or court that has re-

tained me can rapidly move to dismiss either the questionable testimony or the claim or defense as a whole that is founded on such testimony (*Mayotte M. Jones v. Metrowest Medical Inc.* (CA-96-10860-WD).

By researching via the Internet, an attorney seeking an expert can avoid both false starts and subsequent disappointments. The Internet offers the following advantages for evaluating the potential usefulness of a medical expert in light of the general principles of *Daubert:*

1. *Reliability:* The medical expert needs to be both a practicing physician who consults to other physicians and patients, and well published in refereed medical journals. This information can be gleaned from the expert's Web page more easily than from the c.v. alone. The Web page will often include not only a complete c.v., but also selected case citations and authored publications. Moreover, the expert with a resource page on the Web is more likely to be able to do computer-aided literature searches. Such research can provide the foundation for the reviews and analysis needed to corroborate the reliability of another expert's opinion. In addition, such research can identify alternative opinions in the medical community.
2. *Relevance:* The medical expert needs to show ability to teach not only other medical professionals but also an ability to teach other professionals and educated laypersons, for example, judges, attorneys, and jurors. The attorney can have some sense of how the expert teaches in a public context by reviewing the expert's Web page. The fact that an expert has a content-filled, yet user-friendly Web page can itself be an indication that an expert has the competence, confidence, and sensitivity to present work in a public context with authority rather than arrogance, and in a relevant and meaningful manner.

## Discussion Forums

Internet mailing lists and newsgroups are both excellent tools for identifying and contacting experts. For example, if you practice personal injury law, you may need someone familiar with ski-boot construction. You might try posting to one of the skiing mailing lists or newsgroups or perhaps find out whether competitors of the boot manufacturer in question have online sites (try an AltaVista search).

For any topic you can imagine, there is a listserv, newsgroup, or both available. You usually need to subscribe to a mailing list to post to it, and some lists limit subscribers to those with particular credentials. But many lists have no subscriber limitations at all. An easy way to find whether a list in a particular subject area exists, to find out about any subscriber limitations, or to simply find out how to subscribe is to consult a listserv directory such as Tilenet (http://tile.net/listserv/) or LawLists (http://www.lib.uchicago.edu/~llou/lawlists/info.html). Newsgroups are also excellent sources in the search for experts. Tilenet, LawLists, and Liszt (http://www.liszt.com/news/) feature newsgroup directories.

Once you locate an appropriate discussion forum, the best thing to do is lurk around a bit. In other words, read the messages posted to the list before submitting messages of your own. In this way, you may come across an expert or another lawyer you wish to correspond with. You can then send private e-mail to those individuals, rather than letting all list subscribers know your intentions.

Another anonymous way to gather information on experts is to run searches using DejaNews (http://www.dejanews.com). You can search thousands of newsgroups this way, by subject or keyword (including a particular expert's name). This is an excellent way to attempt to undermine your opponent's expert and even evaluate the reliability of your own expert; you may come across one of the expert's postings that is relevant to the matter at hand.

Access to computer and other technical people is available in profusion online. If you need a computer security expert, someone familiar with setting up a local area network within a law firm, or someone to rebuild a corrupted hard disk, you will find plenty of offers of help if you post a request in one of the relevant newsgroups or mailing lists.

The PSYLAW-L mailing list is a well-trafficked and excellent place to post a request for psychological experts. You can join this group by sending the message "sub PSYLAW-L your name" to listserv@utepa.bitnet

EXPERT-L is an Internet mailing list for individuals engaged in expert witness activities associated with litigation. It was inspired by the need for experts to communicate with each other about issues related to the expert witness profession, such as the following:

- errors and omissions insurance
- dealing with abusive discovery
- dealing with abusive cross-examination
- billing and collection practices
- ethics and professional conduct
- networking with other experts and lawyers

To subscribe, send e-mail to expert-l@lern.mv.com with the word SUBSCRIBE in the subject header.

## EXPERT WITNESS RESOURCES

### Academic Resources

Expert Site Collection—The Northern California Association of Law Libraries offers this compilation of Web sources for expert witnesses. This is an excellent starting point in your expert search. (See Figure 7.3.)

http://www.nocall.org/experts.html

ProfNet—The free Professors Network is based at the State University of New York at Stony Brook and is intended primarily for journalists. However, system operator Dan Forbush indicates that ProfNet will help lawyers locate experts on a case-by-case basis. At ProfNet's core is an e-mail distribution list that enables simultaneous distribution of requests for experts to thousands of public relations directors throughout North America and overseas. The directors represent colleges, universities, and a wide range of academic, government, and corporate entities oriented to schol-

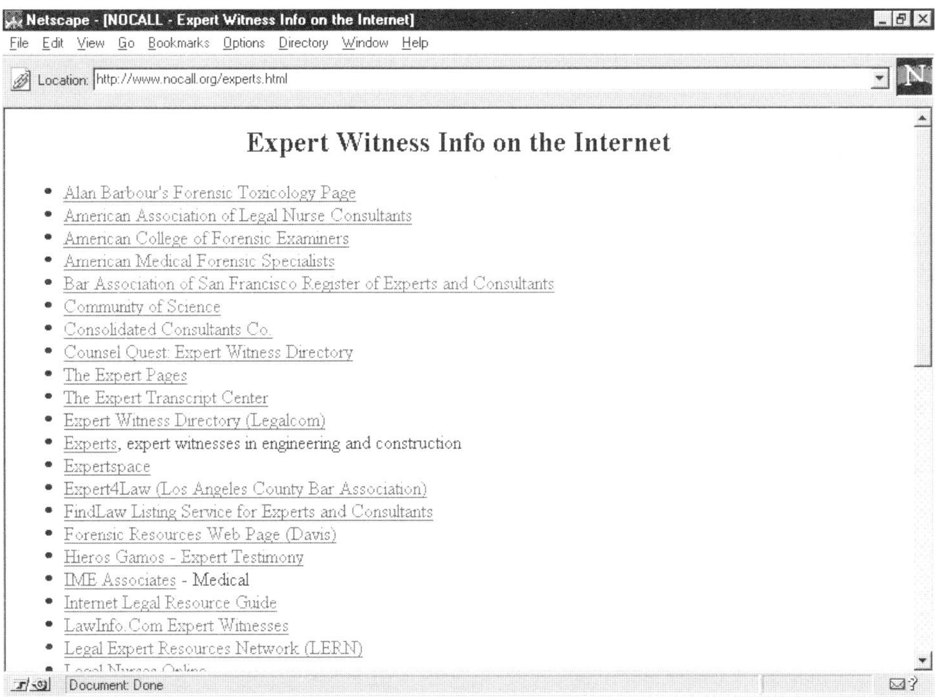


**FIGURE 7.3.** The Northern California Association of Law Libraries offers this excellent starting point in your expert search.

arship and research. Most of the Ivy League and Big Ten schools are represented. Also represented are federal entities, corporate research labs, medical centers, and schools of business and public policy.

http://www.vyne.com/profnet

USC Experts Directory—The University of Southern California provides this listing of more than one thousand USC scientists, scholars, and physicians.

http://www.usc.edu/dept/News_Service/experts_directory.html

Washburn University School of Law Expert Collection

http://lawlib.wuacc.edu/washlaw/expert/expert.html

### Commercial Resources

There are many expert directories on the Internet. Most of them charge experts to be listed, and they provide free search access to everyone. Following is a sampling of the directories available.

Expert Pages—Experts are listed by specialty, country, and U.S. state.

http://www.expertpages.com/

Legal Research Network (LERN)—Provides an expert witness CV database. Researchers pay ninety-nine dollars per year to access the database. Experts pay nothing to be listed. LERN also maintains a free Web site directory of experts who pay ninety-nine dollars per year to be linked to the site.

http://www.witness.net/

National Directory of Expert Witnesses—This very extensive book and searchable online database is produced by the Claims Providers of America. It is designed to be used by law firms and insurance professionals. Experts are arranged into four hundred categories.

http://www.claims.com/

Noble Directory of Experts

http://www.catalog.com/experts/index.html

Referrals—National Consultant Referrals is a membership organization (more than six thousand members) that makes free referrals to its members.

http://www.referrals.com/

Yearbook of Experts, Authorities, and Spokespersons—This is a very extensive searchable database designed primarily for journalists (and also available in book form).

http://www.yearbooknews.com

Yahoo's Expert Witness Collection

http://www.yahoo.com/Business_and_Economy/Companies/Law/Consulting/Expert_Witnesses/

## Deposition Transcript Services

Evidence Technologies—Specializes in medical expert deposition transcripts.

http://www.evidence.com/HTML/experts.html

National Expert Transcript Service

http://www.netscripts.com/input.htm

# CHAPTER EIGHT

# How to Find People on the Net

COMPUTERS ARE INCREDIBLY USEFUL TOOLS if you are looking for someone and slightly scary if you are concerned about personal privacy. The fact is that information about each of us is scattered among countless computer files held by government and private organizations throughout the world. Since we have already disclosed that data, it is impossible to recall. To protect our personal privacy, the most useful thing we can do is be aware of the power of digital communications and cautious about what personal data we release.

But if you are looking for someone, maybe because they owe you money or because an estate you are administering owes them money, or simply to invite them to a reunion, computers make the process easy, even fun. There are several commercial databases available, including Information America and CDB Infotek, that pull together all sorts of records, including voter registration data, motor vehicle registrations, real estate transaction records, and the like, enabling you to discover perhaps far more than you need to know about the person you seek. Using these databases incurs costs that can be significant.

Frequently for free, you can walk into government offices, like the local court house, and search for individuals among the historic records. These records are not always automated, and especially if you do not know the idiosyncracies of the courthouse records, you will need to spend a good deal of time and may end up with a nagging sense that the records may be incomplete.

There is nothing as convenient or as cheap as using the Internet to search for people. Many free databases are available on the Net, and these databases enable you to search throughout the country and offshore as well, if need be. This is not to say that the Net provides access to all records. For example, there are no comprehensive historic court records on the Net. If you wanted to search for litigants in all reported state or federal court decisions, for example, you would be better off using LEXIS or WESTLAW. But if you want to search the nation's phone books or listings of e-mail addresses or recent public company filings or book authors, you cannot do much better than using the Internet.

The Net is also an excellent source for people finding if you know something about the individual. For example, if you are looking for a lawyer, there are two comprehensive American lawyer directories available free on the Net: West's Legal Directory and Martindale Hubbell. If you are looking for an American physician, the American Medical Association provides a database that can locate a doctor by name, specialty, and location from over 650,000 physicians licensed to practice in the United States. In addition, private companies, universities, and other entities provide staff directories online, so if you know that the person you seek is on the faculty at Rutgers University, you can use the Net to find a way to contact that person even when nobody is answering the telephone at the university's main number.

The Net provides some people-finding methods that you can get elsewhere (for example, you can purchase your own nationwide telephone directory on CD-ROM) and some sources that are completely unique (public online access to university faculty directories are not available elsewhere). However, the convenience, perpetual availability, and negligible cost of using the Net to find people make it a logical first choice, even if you end up accessing a fee-based database later. It is often a good idea to try the Net first.

## ■ SUCCESS STORY: CATHY PENNINGTON PAUNOV

Even when you do not know the name of the person you seek, the Net can be the answer to your problem. Lawyer and law librarian Cathy Pennington Paunov tells this story:

> One of my favorite examples is the case where someone in Ohio was working on a salmonella ice cream case. She was desperate. She needed additional information. We wanted to get hold of only practitioners who had worked on cases like this. So I went to AltaVista, which is my favorite search engine on the Internet, and searched the Web for the following three words: *salmonella* and *ice cream*. I got something like three hundred hits. One of them, and it was in the first batch—the nice thing about AltaVista is it ranks the stuff in order of probable relevance. The third or fourth hit down was some law firm in Chicago. Their Web site

said that one of their senior litigation partners had handled the largest salmonella ice cream case in the country. I actually picked up the phone because I knew how desperate this poor attorney was. I picked up the phone and called the attorney in Ohio and said, listen, here's someone in Chicago. I also called the Chicago attorney and warned him I was doing this—and he said fine, I'd be happy to help her out.

I don't think I would have found the salmonella ice cream guy but for the Internet. There's no way I could have found him anywhere else. That was the most incredible story. I've got one very happy small town lawyer, and she's got the name of the top legal expert in the field. ■

## White Pages

The most common (though often overlooked) way to find people is to use the most common reference book there is: the white pages. The thousands of U.S. regional phone directories are perfectly suited to the quick lookup speed of computer databases. Some years ago, a number of CD-ROM publishers seized the opportunity to issue national phone directories on disk. The Internet starts where the CD-ROM companies stopped and takes off from there.

Net phone books are a step ahead of CD-ROM phone books in many ways. The Net makes databases easier to update and distribute, so they can be more current than CD-ROM, although it is hard to tell how often the Net-based directories are updated. Using the Net avoids the need to change CD-ROM disks. Net phone books are accessible from anywhere, and, of course, Net phone books are free. On the flip side, if you want to print large phone lists, CD-ROM is superior. Net-based directories generally allow you to display only a few name-phone listings at a time. If you are attempting to print a large list, you will be better off using CD-ROM.

There is a good deal of similarity among the Web-based phone books. Many of them draw data from the same source. Database America, a privately held firm based in New Jersey, is a major supplier of directory data. (See Figure 8.1.) Another similarity is that nearly all of the phone book sites are advertiser supported. There are also notable differences among the sites. Some provide e-mail as well as phone number data, while others do not. Some provide business listings as well as residential numbers. Some of the sites offer special features, including zip code lookup or reverse phone number searches.

One of the most commonly used phone directories on the Net is provided by the Four11 Corporation (http://www.four11.com/). The Four11 phone directory is a U.S. nationwide phone number database compiled

**FIGURE 8.1.** Most of the phone books on CD-ROM and the Web get their data from the marketing information company Database America. The firm has its own people- and business-finder site. It is one the few sites that still provides a reverse phone number lookup feature.

from published white page directories and other publicly available sources. Simply enter a name, city, and state (the city and state are not required but will speed the search) and hit the search button. Results usually include street address, telephone number, and sometimes an e-mail address. If Four11 does not turn up the number you seek, you might try one of the other free phone books on the Net. Each white page directory has its own search tool, so you will frequently get different results depending on where you search.

## WHITE PAGES RESOURCES

### Basic Directories

Bigfoot Directory—Over 100 million listings.

http://www.bigfoot.com/

Database America—This site has a crisscross feature. If you type in a phone number, you will get back a name and address. Some of the other

Net phone directories, including Four11, note that they have discontinued this service because of privacy concerns.

http://www.databaseamerica.com/html/index.htm

Four11— Uses a database from Metromail.

http://www.four11.com/

InfoSpace—Contains 112 million listings. In addition to the usual white pages lookup, InfoSpace links directly to a very flexible map displaying the location of the subject's address as well as all surrounding streets. Click on the subject's address to get directions to the subject's location and a list of surrounding area businesses that fit your criteria (local restaurants, for example). Click on the phone number, hold your phone mouthpiece to your computer speaker, and InfoSpace will send out the tones to dial the number. (Pretty cool!) InfoSpace draws data from the Pro CD database. (See Figure 8.2.)

http://www.infospace.com/

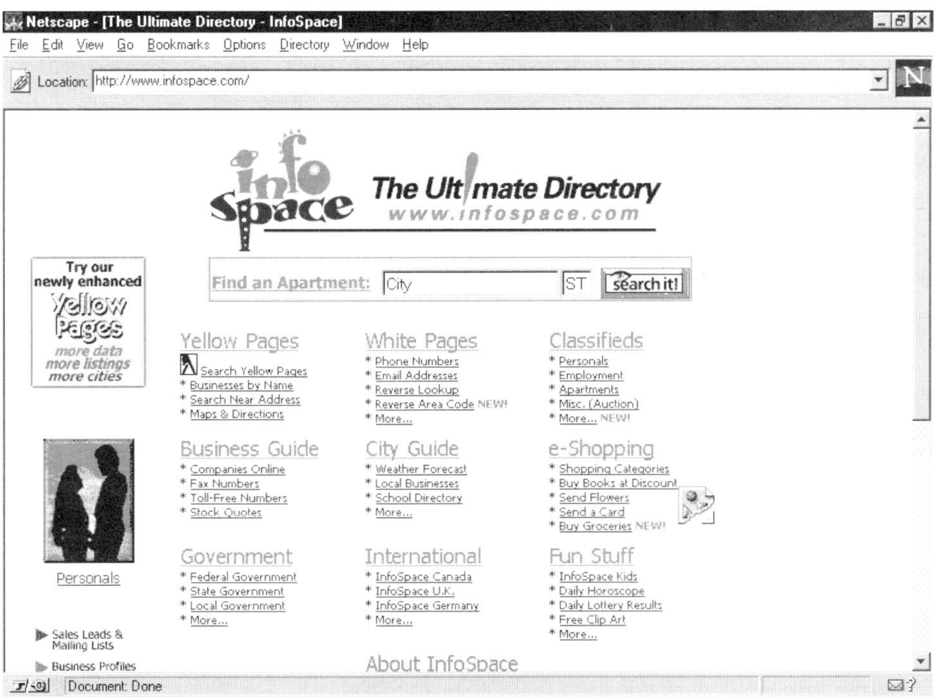


**FIGURE 8.2.** InfoSpace is one of the most interesting and accurate white pages on the Web. It offers a broad collection of directories, including residential, business, international, and government listings, and even a celebrity lookup service.

Switchboard—Contains 93 million listings. This is one of the fastest phone directories on the Web. Switchboard offers an advanced search feature that enables you to select from several dozen affiliations, so that you can search within a group or organization. Affiliation choices include the American Association of Retired Persons, America Online, and the YWCA.

http://www.switchboard.com/

U.S. West—Contains 70 million listings.

http://yp.uswest.com/

WhoWhere—Like Database America, WhoWhere provides a reverse phone number search. This site also enables searching on personal characteristics (choose the Communities advanced search option), including school, occupation, religion, favorite music, and so forth. The site is available in Spanish and French as well as good old English.

http://www.whowhere.com

### Multiple Directories

People Search—Searches four white page directories at once. Requires that you use a browser that supports frames.

http://www.w3com.com/psearch/

Search.com—CNET provides an A–Z list of white page directories.

http://www.search.com/

Trackem

http://www.toolcity.net/~richreen/trackem.html

Ultimate White Pages—Enables searching several phone books (one at a time) from one page.

http://www.theultimates.com/white/

### International Phone Books

WorldPages

http://www.worldpages.com/text/global.html

Yahoo's Regional Collection

http://www.yahoo.com/Reference/White_Pages/Individuals/Regional/

### E-mail Directories

Internet Address Finder—Allows you to search for e-mail address by name, or for name by e-mail address. Lists some 6 million e-mail addresses.

http://www.iaf.net/

Usenet Address Database—Search by name of person or by the organization that provides the person's Net access. This database includes more than 4 million addresses collected from Usenet postings between July 1991 and February 1996.

http://usenet-addresses.mit.edu/

Netpages—This international directory includes more than twenty thousand e-mail addresses. The site does not collect addresses randomly; all entries are volunteered and verified every six months.

http://www.aldea.com/whitepages/white.html

Many of the phone directories listed above also provide e-mail directories.

E-mail Finding Strategy—This site provides a guide to strategies for finding e-mail addresses on the Net.

http://www.qucis.queensu.ca/FAQs/e-mail/finding.html

## *Personal Characteristics*

The more you know about the people you are looking for, the easier it will be to find them. It is generally particularly important to know the proper spelling of the person's full name, including middle name or initial. Other useful details include where the person last resided, where he or she last worked, and his or her birth date and Social Security number. Personal characteristics are very useful when distinguishing among several people with the same relatively common name. Knowing that John F. Smith was born in 1950 and last resided in Lawrence, Kansas, will help distinguish him from the many other John F. Smiths.

We all have many other personal aspects that can be used to find us. We may be lawyers or have other professional affiliations. The Net provides several excellent professional directories. If you know where the target person went to school, there are several alumni directories online, although most of these include self-entered data, meaning schools are not generally posting alumni directories.

## PERSONAL CHARACTERISTICS RESOURCES

### Campaign Donors

Federal Candidate Campaign Money Page—This is a remarkable, free source of data from the Federal Election Commission. You can download the entire soft-dollar contributor database (more than forty thousand names) or simply use this Web page to locate soft- and hard-dollar contributors by name, employer, and zip code. The page also links to political action committee Web pages.

http://www.tray.com/FECInfo/index.html-ssi

### Family Members

Adoptee Resources—The Webgator site pulls together links to several adoption-related pages. Most of these sites are designed for adoptees and birth parents seeking to reunite with each other. Links are provided to adoptive rights associations, to databases of individuals seeking reunion, and to guidance for those searching for family members.

http://www.inil.com/users/dguss/gator9.htm

Ancestor Index—The FamilyFinder Index includes some 115 million names drawn from census, marriage, Social Security, land, and other state and federal records. The site claims that "approximately 20 percent of all individuals who have ever lived in the United States are in our Family-Finder Index."

http://www.familytreemaker.com/ffilink2.html

Death Database—The Social Security Death Index provides vital information for 51 million deceased Americans. Nearly 98 percent of the entire index contains individuals who died after 1962 (when the Social Security Administration began keeping the database on computer). After a successful search in the Death Master File, which results in the individual's birth and death date, Social Security number, and death state, you can request a birth or death certificate. Many entries in the Death Master File have zip codes listed for last-known residence. This site also includes an early

American marriage database, listing nearly seventy-five thousand American marriages before 1800.

http://www.ancestry.com/

Find-a-Grave—Search by name, location, and claim to fame.

http://www.findagrave.com/

Genealogy Links—This page provides a massive (more than twenty-two-thousand-item) collection of genealogy-related Web site links.

http://www.oz.net/~cyndihow/sites.htm

National Archives—The National Archives and Records Administration (NARA) does not provide direct access to any databases here, but this site does detail NARA holdings and provide guidance in genealogy research.

http://www.nara.gov/genealogy/

### Federal Government and Military Personnel

MilitaryCity Online—Provided by the private firm Army Times Publishing Company, this site provides access to a database of 10 million active, reserve, retired, and veteran military personnel, though access costs four dollars per month.

http://www.militarycity.com/

Collection—Webgator features an extensive collection of military- and government-related Web sites. Most of these links provide contact information for government facilities (including U.S. embassies and federal agencies) and also describe the procedures required to get information about members of the U.S. military. There is not much here in terms of actual data on individuals, although, again, the site does tell you how to access such data.

http://www.inil.com/users/dguss/gator69.htm

Congresspeople—Allows you to enter your zip code and find your representatives.

http://congress.nw.dc.us/congressorg/search.shtml

Federal Government Directory

http://bp.fed.gov/main.html

NASA Personnel Directory—This is a searchable database of seemingly all staff at the National Aeronautics and Space Administration's many facilities. Data provided includes phone number and postal and e-mail addresses.

http://x500.ksc.nasa.gov/x500.html

Veterans—This is a database of some six thousand self-submitted military veterans.

http://www.wavenet.com/~beerborn/index.html

## Prison Inmates

Federal Bureau of Prisons—Pursuant to the Freedom of Information Act (5 USC 552) and the Privacy Act of 1974 (5 USC 552a), anyone can receive information about federal inmates (defined as those convicted of violating federal law). Available information includes name, age, register number, and sentencing and confinement data (offense, date sentenced, institution of confinement, and so forth). Information on federal inmates confined from 1982 to the present is available from the national Inmate Locator (202-307-3126). Information on federal inmates confined before 1982 is available from the Office of Communications and Archives (202-307-2934). This Web page provides a list of all the federal prison facilities, grouped according to level of security.

http://www.bop.gov/

## Professionals

Florida Professional Licensees—The State Department of Business and Professional Regulation provides this free database, allowing you to search for licensees and business names by occupation or license number. Occupations listed include accountant, architect, auctioneer, contractor, engineer, and many more.

http://fcn.state.fl.us/oraweb/owa/dbpr2.qry_lic_menu

New York Professional Licenses—The New York State Department of Education provides access to licensing and disciplinary action data for professionals, including architects, chiropractors, accountants, physicians, engineers, and so forth.

http://www.nysed.gov/prof/profhome.htm

Lawyers—Martindale Hubbell is one of the best-known lawyer directories. West's Legal Directory lists 800,000 profiles of lawyers and law firms in the United States and Canada. If you do not find the lawyer you need using Martindale Hubbell or West's, Findlaw provides a comprehensive collection of most of the lawyer directories on the Net.

http://www.martindale.com/

http://www.wld.com/

http://www.findlaw.com/14firms/index.html

Lawyers Who Have Been Disciplined—Misconduct.com has a searchable database of attorneys who have been disciplined for professional misconduct, unethical behavior, or both.

http://www.misconduct.com/

Physicians—The American Medical Association's *Physician Select* option lists all accredited doctors in the United States (more than 650,000). Additional information available here includes address, phone number, specialty, where degree was obtained, and where residency was served.

http://www.ama-assn.org/

Writers—Search the Library of Congress and other publication catalogs.

http://lcweb.loc.gov/z3950/gateway.html#lc

### School Alumni

World AlumniNet—This site appears to offer a collection of international and U.S. college alumni directories. However, it seems that the directories are based on personally supplied listings. As a result, the site is not at all comprehensive and a hit-or-miss proposition for finding people, at best.

http://www.infophil.com/World/Alumni/

ClassMates Online—This is another example of a self-inclusive database. The site claims people have added their names from "more than 20,000 high schools covering all 50 states, Canada, and about 300 American/ Canadian territorial and overseas high schools."

http://www.classmates.com/

### Shareholders

Commercial (that is, non-Internet, fee-based) databases provide access to Secretary of State corporate affiliation databases and other sources that help identify people based on their employment by and ownership interest in companies. Shareholder records are also helpful sources for learning about people. You will not find such lists on the Net, but you can find information on how to access such records. Click over to http://www.itlnet.com/ moneypages/syndicate/stocks/sec/index.html for an explanation of how to access shareholder lists and many more documents provided by the Securities and Exchange Commission.

### Vehicle Owners

Driver's license and vehicle registration information is an excellent way to find people of legal driving age. Driver's licenses are common pieces of identification, and most people have one. Although a few states have laws restricting public access to driving and vehicle registration records, most states still provide easy access to this data. Commercial databases like CDB Infotek provide access to driver's license and vehicle data, but very little if any is available free on the Net. Searching vehicle registrations is a better way to find people than searching driver's licenses, because registrations are renewed annually, while driver's licenses are renewed less frequently.

You will need two pieces of information to search motor vehicle records: the subject's name and a date of birth. The date of birth is especially important if your subject has a common name. If you have those two pieces of information, the motor vehicle department can usually provide a current address; last known address; personal information, such as height, weight, and eye and hair color; previous names, if any; the numbers and types of vehicles owned by that person; and any traffic tickets the person may have accumulated in recent years.

Motor vehicle accident data is a potential gold mine of information. If lawsuits were filed due to an accident, there is no telling what interesting things you can discover. The motor vehicle department can tell you where the accident happened. Use that information to identify the local jurisdiction, where you can retrieve a copy of the police report that may have been filed.

Article on Using Vehicle Registration to Find People

http://www.facsnet.org/report_tools/findem_fast/vehicle_reg.html

Complete List of Driver's License Bureaus

http://www.facsnet.org/report_tools/findem_fast/list.html

DMV and Property Records from Search Milwaukee

http://www.ci.mil.wi.us/assessment.htm

Massachusetts' Registry of Motor Vehicles—One of the first departments to put up a Web site that allows interactivity. The site allows online payment of tickets and registration. It does not, however, allow searching of its driver or vehicle registration database on the Net.

http://www.state.ma.us/rmv/

State of Texas Licensed Drivers—Fee required.

http://www.publicdata.com/

## Finding Forwarding Information

When people change their name, address, phone number, e-mail account, or URL, it can sometimes be difficult to track them down. The Net is not great at providing forwarding information. A solution to this problem is provided by the Semaphore Corporation (http://www.semaphorecorp.com/default.html). A database called Where Did They Go? lets you search for people who have moved or changed their name and for phone numbers that have changed. The data is drawn from direct submissions to Semaphore and from address corrections received from the Postal Service or online services. This database is also useful for finding companies that have moved or changed names.

Semaphore also offers a National Address Browser. This is described as "a complete postal database with CASS-certified address correction software." You can browse through all U.S. addresses, zip codes, and mail carrier route numbers.

## Backgrounding People

In addition to finding people you once knew or would like to know— like the lawyer who's handled salmonella ice cream cases—the Internet is an excellent way to get background information on people. For example, if you are about to depose an expert witness, one way to dig into that expert's past is to see whether he or she has been talking in any of the Internet newsgroups. The sixteen thousand or so newsgroups, which cover every subject you can imagine, are easily accessible on the Web via DejaNews at http://www.dejanews.com/. (See Figure 8.3.)

You can search DejaNews, using the expert's name, to see if he or she is mentioned or if he or she has posted any comments. In this way, if you are incredibly lucky, you might discover the expert discussing the very subject on which you plan to depose him or her, or you might find the expert making disclosures that could be useful to you during the deposition. If you are able to locate a posting made by your expert, you can use DejaNews to get a profile of the expert. Just click on the expert's e-mail address as it appears in the DejaNews display, and you will be presented with a report listing the number of newsgroup postings made by the expert over the past two years, and the newsgroups to which the expert has posted.

**FIGURE 8.3.** DejaNews makes it particularly easy to read and post to newsgroups.

**FIGURE 8.4.** Reference.com makes it easy to search through and participate in several hundred thousand newsgroups, mailing lists, and Web forums.

Another free newsgroup search service that also searches Internet mailing lists is Reference.Com (**http://www.reference.com**). (See Figure 8.4.) This service alerts you whenever anyone posts a message to a newsgroup or mailing list that mentions a word or phrase that you have provided. Using the Active Queries function, you can store queries on Reference.com's machine, and these queries will execute daily. For example, you might want to know every time your subject posts to any newsgroup. To access this service, you need to provide your e-mail address and choose a password.

When looking for background information on people, it can also be worthwhile to simply search for your subject's name using Internet search engines. It is possible that your subject has authored documents on the Web or perhaps is mentioned in someone else's document. For the relatively short amount of time it will take to type the name into the search window and scan through the responses, this approach may prove surprisingly worthwhile. This sort of approach is likely to be most productive if the person you seek has some level of notoriety.

## Other Options

### Periodical Sources

In this chapter we have taken a look at broad-based directories and public record sources. Another way to look for an individual is to check periodicals and newspapers. Sometimes, when you cannot find someone any other way, you may find they have been mentioned in an article that provides a key piece of information.

A broad-based search using an Internet search engine is somewhat akin to a broad periodical search on the NEXIS or DIALOG commercial database services. Both types of searches examine an enormous range of documents. One of the primary distinctions between using the Net and the commercial services is the historic archive held on the commercial services. Due in part to the Internet's youth and publishers' struggle to find a balance between free and fee-based material, there is a limited amount of historic periodical data on the Net. But there is some.

The Net provides free access to a few weeks' or months' worth of major news media, including wire services and the business press. One of the best searchable collections of free Internet news databases is the Internet Sleuth (http://isleuth.com). This site provides access to some eighteen hundred Net databases, which you can search individually or all at once.

To find the Internet location of newspapers, magazines, and radio or TV stations, consider the American Journalism Review Newslink site (http://www.newslink.org/) or Editor & Publisher Interactive (http://www.mediainfo.com/). Consult "How to Get News on the Net," Chapter 6 in this book for more on news sources.

### Public Records

Privacy legislation in the United States is currently focused on the public sector. Although there is legislation protecting privately held data in random niches, including the Robert Bork–inspired Video Privacy Protection Act (which protects from public scrutiny the lists of videotapes we rent), most private data is protected only by the discretion of the private entities that possess it. Public data, on the other hand, including our tax records and the FBI's national criminal database, are protected from public disclosure by the Privacy Act of 1974. As a result, plenty of rich governmentally held data that could be used to find people and find out about people is unavailable to the public.

There are also troves of governmentally held data that *must* be made available to the public in order to, for example, advance commerce. Real estate indices, for example, need to be available to enable the free transfer of property. Public data like real estate records, motor vehicle information, and the like are the best place to search for someone, after searching the privately held records held by phone companies and other organizations.

An important distinction between publicly and privately owned data is that the government is not as motivated as the private sector to make optimum use of the data. As a result, the enormous data collections held by federal, state, and local governments are often not in electronic form. To further complicate accessing public data via the Net, of those public records that have been digitized, only a small portion are available free online. Keep in mind, then, that the Net can be a useful source for public record research, but a comprehensive search will also involve using commercial databases and physically traveling to courthouses and other archives to review paper records.

## PUBLIC RECORDS RESOURCES

Freedom of Information—This page details how to obtain information under state and federal freedom-of-information laws. It includes details on each state's laws and various relevant links.

http://reporters.net/nfoic/web/index.htm

Public Records Source—KnowX provides free real property, "adverse filings," and several other searches on individuals and businesses. Adverse filings involve bankruptcies, judgments, liens, lawsuits, and Uniform Commercial Code filings (UCCs). Free results are highly summarized; for example, "Joe Smith is a plaintiff in a suit filed in New York." You will pay between $2.50 and $9.00 for a more detailed record. Data provided here are drawn from the Information America database.

http://www.knowx.com/

Social Security Number Validation—This site also indicates when and where the Social Security number was issued.

http://www.informus.com/ssnlkup.html

Vital Records Information—Vital records are those involving life events—births, marriages, deaths. This site identifies, by state and county, the sources, procedures, and costs involved in retrieving vital records.

http://www.inlink.com/~nomi/vitalrec/staterec.html

## Getting Help

The Information Professionals Listserv (INFOPRO) is subscribed to by private investigators, public records researchers, investigative reporters, and lots of other folks who collectively have lots of ideas and expertise regarding finding people. Access to the list is regulated. To apply for access, send e-mail to James Cook (jcook@netcom.com).

# CHAPTER NINE

# How to Research Companies on the Net

COMPANY RESEARCH IS ONE OF THE SUBJECTS that ought to be taught in law school. There are endless bits of information that lawyers need to know about companies in order to serve clients. Understanding what information is available and how to access it efficiently can make all the difference, whether you are bringing suit, seeking to help your client acquire a company, or representing shareholders.

For example, if your client has been injured by an improperly designed garage door, you need to figure out who the proper defendant is. Is your target the manufacturer identified on the door itself? Is that company the parent corporation, or merely a subsidiary? Where is the company headquarters? In Delaware or in the United Kingdom?

Counsel to shareholder groups may need access to corporate press releases or all recent SEC filings or corporate annual reports. If your business clients seek to acquire a firm, you may be asked to locate sales figures, which can be particularly difficult to find for small private companies.

The Internet can help with all these tasks. If you are searching for a company's address but you are uncertain how to spell the company name, there are Internet directories (for example, http://www.companylink.com/) that enable you to search based on the type of industry and state where the company is headquartered. Such directories can also be used to determine quickly whether your client's proposed company name is in use anywhere in the country.

While the existence of a company with the same name your client plans to use for a new venture or product does not necessarily bar use of the name, a quick, free Internet search of a business phone book may save a more involved and expensive trademark or trade name search. Such directories also allow you to search at your own pace through the nation's business phone books, a luxury previously available only to those willing to spend time in the rare library that keeps current phone books for the nation, or to those willing to pay the cost of a national phone book on CD-ROM.

## *Where to Start*

Company Web sites are often the simplest starting points for company research. Company sites generally provide information about products and services, press releases, and other news that can be useful in investigations. If you simply need to know the Web address, phone number, address, or proper spelling of a company, try one of the phone book pages.

Company sites often begin where company literature leaves off. Companies may take printed literature and transform it into an expanded electronic dossier, offering more insight into products and activities. A good example of this is provided by the Bay State Gas Company (http://www.bgc.com/bgc/). This site offers press releases, financial reports, consumer information, new initiatives being worked on, and much more.

For another example, browse the home pages of the international marketing research firm Find/SVP (http://www.findsvp.com) and take a look at the electronic database of market research reports as well as the descriptions of services. Another marketing research firm, Dataquest, takes a similar approach (http://www.dataquest.com).

Internet subject guides are also good places to start company research. When using these guides—for example, the Yahoo Guide (http://www.yahoo.com/) and Galaxy (http://www.einet.net/galaxy.html)—try categories like Business & Commerce, Corporations, Companies, Business & Economics, or Business & Finance. Also consider industry categories relevant to your target company.

### BUSINESS PHONE BOOK RESOURCES

AT&T Internet Toll-Free 800 Directory

http://www.tollfree.att.net/

Bigbook—Search through 16 million listings.

http://www.bigbook.com/

BigYellow

http://bigyellow.com/

Company Fax Lookup

http://www.555-1212.com/fax_us.htm

GTE Superpages—Enables reverse searching (entering the phone number to find the business).

http://yp.gte.net/

Multiple Business Phone Books—This page pulls together several databases, including the Switchboard Directory, AT&T Directory, and GTE Interactive Yellow Pages.

http://www.companylink.com/phone.cfm

SalesLeads USA—American Business Information enables free searching through more than 14 million yellow page listings.

http://www.abii.com/

Domain Name Lookup—A truly unique-to-the-Internet source for finding companies is the Internet Network Information Center (InterNic) database of registered domain names. The Netpartners Company Site Locator enables you to search for corporate Web pages using the InterNic list of registered domain names. (See Figure 9.1.) The InterNic site is another, though less elegant, access point for the same data.

http://netpart.com/company/

http://rs.internic.net/cgi-bin/whois

Major Corporations—Quick links to the sites of many large corporations.

http://www.cio.com/WebMaster/competition.html

Networth—More corporate sites.

http://networth.galt.com/www/home/equity/irr/

**FIGURE 9.1.** The Netpartners Company Site Locator searches the InterNic database to find company Web sites.

## *Public Company Starting Points*

An important distinction to make when setting out to conduct company research is whether the target is public (meaning shares in the company are traded on a public exchange) or private (meaning shares in the firm are not publicly traded). There is much more credible information available about public companies than about private firms.

Public companies are regulated by the federal Securities and Exchange Commission and are therefore required to make certain public filings, many of which are easily retrievable on the Net for free via the EDGAR database (http://www.sec.gov/cgi-bin/srch-edgar).

The following section lists a few excellent sites that provide links to public companies. There are a number of sites on the Net that list companies that pay a fee for being listed. This practice limits the number of firms that appear on any given Web page. Generally, such sites are not included in the following descriptions.

## PUBLIC COMPANY RESOURCES

Wall Street Research Network—This site lists not only U.S. public companies but also Canadian companies whose shares trade on the Toronto, Vancouver, Montreal, and Alberta exchanges. This appears to be one of the most comprehensive company sites on the Net. Data presented for each company include links to the company home page and SEC filings, links to company news (courtesy of Yahoo), and lots of information about the company's stock.

http://www.wsrn.com/index.html

Yahoo Company Information—This site is very easy to use. The screen presents scrollable lists of companies. Opposite each company are three options: News, Profiles, or Quote. The News option lists news articles from the past seven days. Yahoo draws its articles from the following news sources: Reuters General News, Reuters Securities News, PR Newswire, Business Wire, and UPI. The Profile option lists the company's address, phone, fax, and top executives. Links are provided to the company home page, stock price, and SEC filings.

http://biz.yahoo.com/news/

Companylink—This site provides cross-indexed access to data on some forty-five thousand U.S. companies. This database, compiled from Hoover's Online and CorpTech, can be searched based on the company name (or portion thereof) or ticker symbol. In addition, you can narrow your search by specifying a primary industry and state. The results presented for each company include the basic contact information as well as the nature of ownership (public versus private). In addition, Companylink provides free links for each company to the home page, stock prices and charts, a local street map and local weather, headlines of all related news stories, and the full text of today's news articles. For an additional fee, you can get the full text of all related news stories and summary profiles (including the CEO, annual sales, and employee count).

http://www.companylink.com/

Major Corporations—This site provides links to several hundred corporate sites and several other domestic and international corporate directories.

http://www.cio.com/central/businesses.html

### Annual Reports

Annual reports are chock full of interesting company information, all shaped and supplied by the company itself. You will usually find a message from the chief executive, a discussion of new initiatives begun in the past year, a list of company executives, and extensive company financials. Anyone can get a copy of a company's annual report by simply calling the corporation's investor relations department.

Examples of companies that post annual reports on the net are Microsoft (http://www.microsoft.com/msft/), Intel (http://www.intel.com/intel/finance/), and Schlumberger (http://www.slb.com/ir/). To find whether a particular company has an annual report on the Internet, try a search engine and search on keywords like the company's name and the words *earnings* or *annual report*.

Generally, however, search engines such as AltaVista, Excite, and Lycos are not the best choices if you are looking for annual reports. The typical search will not find annual report collections on the Web. A better bet is the Public Register's Annual Report Service (PRARS) (http://www.prars.com/). (See Figure 9.2.) PRARS provides free access to a database of some thirty-two hundred public companies. Then, using e-mail from the site, you can request that annual reports be sent to you via postal mail, anywhere in the United States, again for no charge.

Investor Relations Information Network (IRIN) at http://www.irin.com/colist.html does not have a collection as extensive as that of PRARS, but IRIN does supply access to annual reports that users can download in portable document format (PDF)—though be aware that such downloading can take time. More than six hundred companies are currently listed at the IRIN site, and each entry includes basic corporate information, charts and graphs, plus the annual report.

If you are willing to pay for information, check out the Annual Reports Library (http://www.zpub.com/sf/arl/). For a $200 annual fee, members receive unlimited access to the collection of 1.45 million annual reports and proxies from corporations, foundations, banks, mutual funds, and public institutions, covering the past ten years and 150 countries.

Another for-pay annual report service is Brainwave (http://alpha.n2kbrainwave.com/p/p0541cc.htm). Brainwave's advantage is its search capability, which allows users to search for annual reports by company name, ticker symbol, city, state, DUNS number, or subject—a much more focused search tool than one usually sees on the Internet. The cost is four dollars per page.

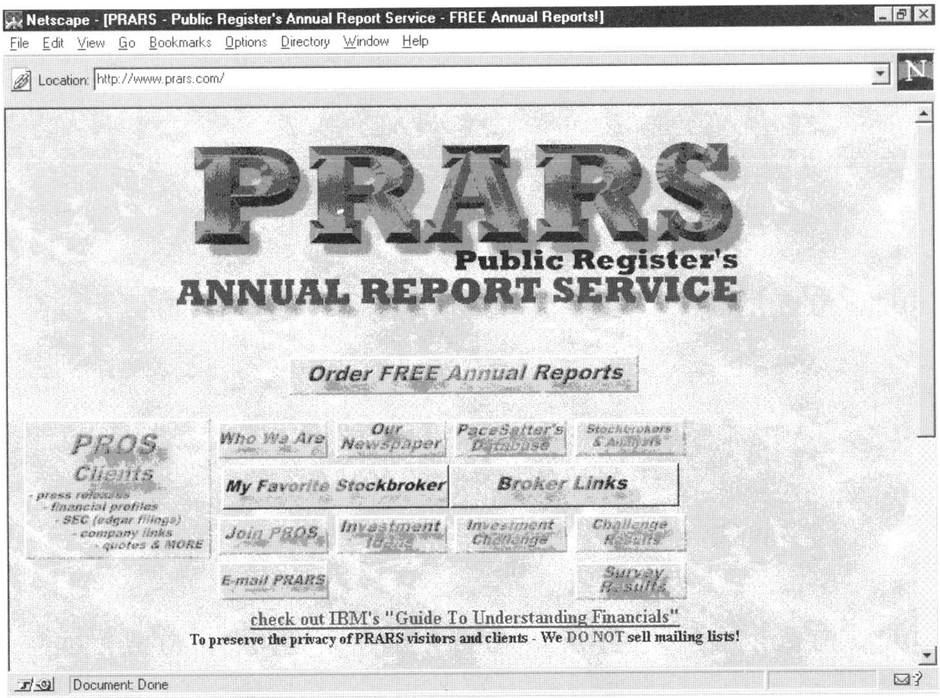


**FIGURE 9.2.** The Public Register's Annual Report Service will send you annual reports via postal mail for free in the United States.

## SEC Filings

The Electronic Data Gathering Analysis and Retrieval (EDGAR) database (http://www.sec.gov/edgarhp.htm) provided by the U.S. Securities and Exchange Commission is by far one of the richest collections of information available concerning U.S. public companies. Although there are many companies that repackage EDGAR data and provide them in nicer formats along with various value-added services, the EDGAR database on the Net, which is completely free of charge, serves many purposes very satisfactorily.

As of May 6, 1996, all public domestic companies are required to make their SEC filings on EDGAR, with very few exceptions. Annual reports to shareholders are not required to be filed electronically, although annual 10-K reports are filed on EDGAR. EDGAR documents are available on the Net within 24 hours after filing.

For public companies, EDGAR provides access to proxy statements. Proxies are sent to public corporation shareholders to solicit votes on corporate governance matters, including election of directors or issuance of additional shares of stock. You can search for proxies in EDGAR by company name or ticker symbol. (A tip: Search for companies by using the *adj* connector. For example, to find International Business Machines, search for *international adj business adj machines.*) The proxy statement will contain information on board members, as will the annual report to shareholders, which is usually Exhibit 13 on the 10-K. Proxy statements can also contain executive compensation information.

## Private Company Starting Points

It can be very difficult to get accurate, timely information about private companies. Private firms are not bound by SEC filing requirements, which result in the rich trove of public company data available on EDGAR. One of the most common sources of private company data, the Dun & Bradstreet Company report, is composed largely of self-reported data, making it hard to know whether the data are completely accurate.

### PRIVATE COMPANY RESOURCES

Hoover's Online—This site provides an excellent collection of information on a limited number of public companies (about ten thousand of them). For $9.95 per month, you can search Hoover's company profiles for insight on more than twenty-six hundred companies in the United States and elsewhere. For free, Hoover's provides capsule profiles on some ten thousand companies. The capsules provide the basics found at many other company database sites, including names of top executives, quarterly financials, a link to the company Web site, and a map showing the street location of the firm. But Hoover's goes a step further, leveraging the Internet in a logical way.

Hoover's links directly to a number of Net search engines, including AltaVista, Excite, and Lycos, and automatically inserts the company name you are investigating into the search engine you choose. If you click on one of the engines listed on the Hoover's page, you will be taken directly to the search results for that company. This speeds up the search process considerably. Hoover's will also search for relevant news stories from its news partners, including CNNfn, Infoseek Guide News, *Fortune, Time, L.A. Times,* and the *Washington Post.* Overall, Hoover's Online is an excellent free Net resource, except for the fact that the number of companies listed is limited.

http://www.hoovers.com/

Dun & Bradstreet—This site provides access to some 100,000 public and private companies. Listings feature annual sales, company size, ownership structure, and Web and e-mail addresses.

http://www.companiesonline.com/

Webgator—This page links to a number of state corporate records offices. Most of these do not yet provide actual corporate data on the Net, although some do link to corporate forms and procedural information.

http://www.inil.com/users/dguss/gator68.htm

## ASSOCIATION RESOURCES

An easy way to find an association's Web site, if you know the name of the association, is simply to enter its name into a Web search engine, like AltaVista. Otherwise, you can try one of the association databases online.

Associations Online—The Internet Public Library provides this collection of more than five hundred links to associations on the Net. You can search by title of association or by category. Categories include arts, business, computers, entertainment, health, industry, labor, law, and science.

http://www.ipl.org/ref/AON/

American Society of Association Executives—This site features several directories of associations.

http://www.asaenet.org/Gateway/GatewayHP.html

Nonprofits Online—You can use this database to search for an organization's Web page by name or browse through the hundreds of listings.

http://www.impactonline.org/listings/index.html

Professional Organizations Index—Directories included are business related: accounting, appraisal, banking, brokerage, entrepreneur, law, and venture capital.

http://www.nvst.com/rsrc/proforg.htm

## NONPROFIT ORGANIZATION RESOURCES

Internet NonProfit Center—Locate nonprofits by searching the Non-Profit Locator database (by keyword, zip code, or state) of more than 1 million nonprofits. The data is drawn from the IRS. In addition, this site houses an extensive collection of links to nonprofit organizations.

http://www.nonprofits.org/

Nonprofit Resource Center—This is a service from John Farino, CPA, who provides some accounting-oriented and introductory information on nonprofits.

http://www.1800net.com/nprc/

Nonprofit Resource Collection

http://www.clark.net/pub/pwalker/General_Nonprofit_Resources/

Sample Nonprofit Bylaws/Articles of Incorporation

Colorado (http://www.fortnet.org/FortNet/bylaws.html)

California (http://www.c4net.org/bylaws.html)

Pennsylvania (http://www.kli.org/kli/KLI.Bylaws.html)

Minnesota (http://www.mncn.org/articles.htm or http://www.mista.org/articles.html)

Indiana (http://www.noblecan.org/appendix1.html)

State Charity Regulators

http://www.gov.state.md.us/sos/charity/html/otstates.html

## OTHER CORPORATE RESOURCES

Corporate Governance

http://www.corpgov.net/

http://www.corpfinet.com/EP_Corp_Gov.html

Corporate Finance Center

http://www.seclaw.com/centers/corpfin.shtml

Corporate Counsel Weekly Summaries from BNA

http://www.bna.com/hub/bna/legal/ccwhigh.html

Guide to Using the Net for Company Research

http://hslc.org/~tyburski/coinfo/steps.htm

Limited Liability Companies

http://www.llc-usa.com/

Mergers and Acquisitions Marketplace—This site provides resources for selling, buying, and investigating businesses.

http://www.mergernetwork.com/default.htm

Merger and Acquisitions/Venture Capital Meta Site—This site houses an extensive collection of merger-and-acquisitions-related links.

http://www.nvst.com/

Public Records—KnowX provides free adverse filings on businesses. Adverse filings involve bankruptcies, judgments, liens, lawsuits, and UCCs. Free results are highly summarized; for example, "Joe Smith is a plaintiff in a suit filed in New York." You will pay between $2.50 and $9.00 for a more detailed record. Data is drawn from the Information America database.

http://www.knowx.com/

Secretary of State Corporate Records—See Figure 9.3.

http://plains.uwyo.edu/~prospect/secstate.htmlx

Thomas Register of American Manufacturers—Search 155,000 U.S. and Canadian companies to find the industrial products or services you need.

http://www2.thomasregister.com/index.html

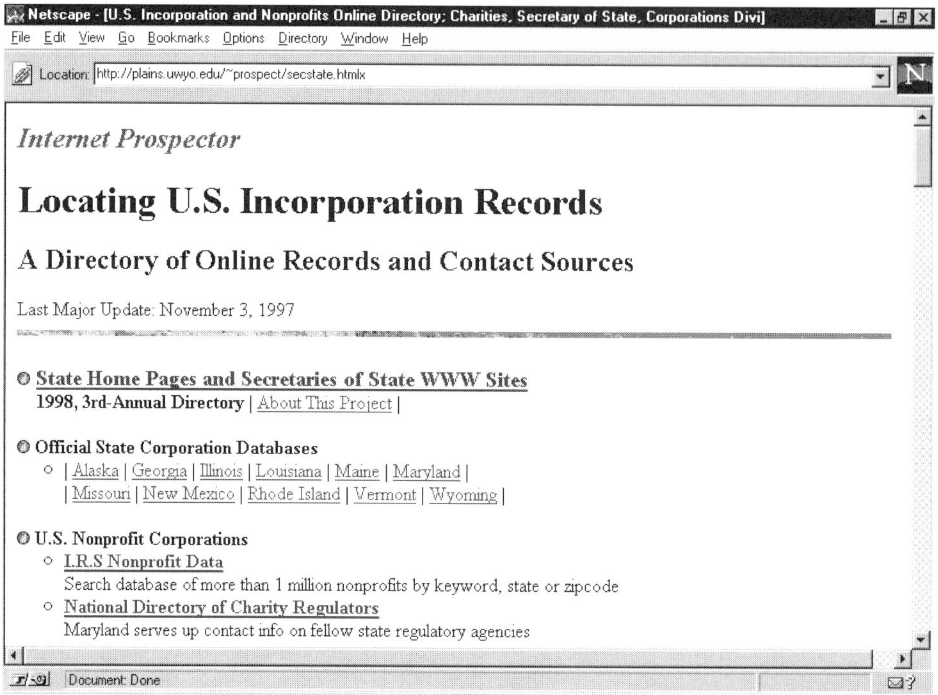


**FIGURE 9.3.** State corporate records are generally held by the secretary of state. This site provides links to many state record offices. In a few cases, you can search state corporate records right on the Net for free (try Alaska).

## News

Finally, the Internet has some of the finest resources available anywhere for current news. In the context of company research, news sources can provide real-world context for the annual reports and financial statements available from the many sources discussed in this chapter. There are many news sources on the Net. For starters, try PR Newswire (**http://www.prnewswire.com/cnoc/acct.html**). Generally, PR Newswire information is fee based, but the Net site provides free instant access to the most current news concerning hundreds of the most active public and private companies. See Chapter Six, "How to Get News on the Net."

*CHAPTER* **TEN**

# How to Conduct Competitive Intelligence on the Net

## What Is Competitive Intelligence?

The cliché definition of competitive intelligence (CI) involves corporate spies who hoodwink rival executives into revealing trade secrets. While corporate espionage does occur, CI is not cloak-and-dagger. Rather, the key element of truly useful competitive intelligence is an analysis of business and legal data, aimed at understanding the competitive environment. Such understanding can alert you and your clients to threats and opportunities. Therefore, CI is essentially carefully collected and analyzed information.

Lawyers typically advise corporate clients to protect trade secrets and corporate assets. An even more productive activity can be the proactive use of business intelligence. For example, knowing that a competitor is test-marketing a product with a brand name very similar to your client's trademark is valuable information. However, also knowing that the competitor has sought to register the mark and that the Patent and Trademark Office has denied the trademark application indicates that there may be a lack of communication between the rival's marketing and legal departments. A strategic conclusion based on this competitive intelligence might be to delay sending a cease and desist letter to the competitor's legal department, to avoid alerting the competitor to the problem with the mark.

Some 10 percent of large corporations have in-house CI departments, which commonly save those companies millions per year. Many corporate executives consider such efforts imperative to survival, especially in the globalized economy. Many smaller companies, however, either cannot afford CI or, more likely, are not savvy enough to recognize its benefits. The lawyer who perceives the worth in CI and takes the time to develop intelligence research skills can provide immense value to clients.

CI can be based on information gleaned from corporate Web sites, obscure publications, government records, and company trash bins. Information gathered can identify new products planned, the percentage of annual revenue spent on computing, and the hiring and layoff trends of select competitors. Good competitive intelligence acts to filter through the ocean of available information to identify and analyze the most relevant facts. CI enables businesses to move beyond merely accessing information to acting on intelligence.

## *Why Use the Internet for Competitive Intelligence?*

It is incumbent on lawyers to ensure their business advice considers all the relevant facts, some of which are discoverable only through careful and comprehensive competitive intelligence research, including use of the Internet. The Net has quite simply become one of the primary tools in a research strategy that aims to pull data from all relevant sources.

As those who have ventured online can attest, the Internet contains a vast collection of information, some of it fascinating and uniquely valuable, and some of it useless. But the sheer volume of data testifies to the Net's value for competitive intelligence; it demands attention by CI researchers. The Internet simply cannot be ignored.

The emergence of the Internet as a critical business (and therefore legal) information tool parallels the rise of CI as an essential offensive and defensive strategic weapon. Both the Net and CI grew from the need for the United States to address international issues. While the Internet was created by the U.S. Department of Defense to provide sustained communication in case of catastrophic war, CI's use by domestic corporations rose in response to foreign competitive threats and the need to penetrate overseas markets. Deregulation of various industries in the United States and elsewhere has also increased competitive pressures and fueled the need for companies to increase their use of CI.

The parallel development of the Net and CI suggests a certain symmetry that makes the Internet a natural CI tool. For example, due to its nonproprietary nature and widespread public accessibility, the Internet is perceived as a source of and place to provide "free" information. Perhaps because of this nonownership, many government bodies, domestic and foreign, have chosen to use the Internet medium as a very low-cost distribution mechanism. Among the information distributed on the Net are many national databases that are perfectly suited to investigating competitive companies. In the United States, the Securities and Exchange Commission database known as EDGAR (Electronic Data Gathering, Analysis, and Retrieval system) at http://www.sec.gov/edgarhp.htm is one of the best examples of this trend. EDGAR is a source of data on domestic public companies, and it contains the 10-K, 10-Q, and shareholder proxy statements filed by every publicly held firm. These documents provide a wealth of financial, operational, and strategic information.

As the Internet has grown up along with the discipline of CI, so has the increasing importance of technology in business. As a result, most major companies have established Web sites that are rich with all sorts of information that companies previously did not make easily accessible to the public. For example, some companies post their internal employee directories and company newsletters. Employee directories can be used to identify the caliber of competitors' staffs, while company newsletters may disclose job openings, which may indicate the areas in which a competitor is planning development.

The Internet provides a wealth of CI source data. Included among those sources are several that are available only on the Net. For example, Internet newsgroups (also known as Usenet groups), which can be searched using DejaNews (http://www.dejanews.com), Digital's AltaVista (http://altavista.digital.com/), or the Infoseek Guide (http://www.infoseek.com/), naturally segment hundreds of thousands of conversations according to subject areas. For example, if you represent a firm that plans to hire a particular acoustic engineer to develop a new technology, and you are charged with investigating how this individual represents herself and whether she can be trusted with trade secrets, you might search the archives of the newsgroups alt.sci.physics.acoustics, comp.dcom.telecom.tech, and rec.audio.pro. Such evidence of the engineer's past conversations and online behavior is not available anywhere but on the Internet.

A final reason to use the Net for CI is that doing so can avoid data collection liability. Since the Net is a publicly accessible source, finding information on it may defeat a claim of data theft, privacy violation, or anticompetitive behavior. For example, a company that acquired a competitor's pricing or market share data might be charged with trade secret theft. However, if that information was found on the competitor's Web site, the defense might argue that one cannot steal what has been given away for free.

In addition, using the Internet to conduct research cannot lead to any meaningful identification of who is conducting research. While Web site owners can identify the originating domain names of those who visit sites, researchers can use third-party providers to conduct research, thereby conducting research in virtual, and legitimate, anonymity.

For example, say I am conducting research from my desk at the research company FIND/SVP (http:///www.findsvp.com) using the Internet access provided by the firm. If I point my Internet browser at the IBM Web site (http://www.ibm.com), the IBM webmaster has the ability to know that someone from findsvp.com has visited ibm.com. The Webmaster cannot know, however, that I personally visited ibm.com, only that someone (or even something, since robot programs commonly visit Web sites) from findsvp.com visited. If, however, I dial into my local Internet service provider, CompuServe, for example, and browse over to ibm.com from the CompuServe computer, the IBM webmaster knows only that someone using CompuServe has visited ibm.com. Since CompuServe has millions of subscribers, accessing IBM from CompuServe is a virtually anonymous thing to do.

In general, every Web site you visit can obtain the following information about you: (1) who your ISP (Internet service provider) is, (2) what country you are from, (3) what software you are using, and (4) what kind of computer you have. With a little programming, it can also sometimes determine your name and e-mail address. For a sampling of the sort of calling card information you are leaving at every site you visit, click over to The Anonymizer (http://www.anonymizer.com). (See Figure 10.1.) This site also enables you to surf the Web anonymously. (For anonymous e-mail, consider an anonymous remailer [http://www.defcon.org/anonymous-remailers.html].) The bottom line is that used wisely, the Internet enables you to conduct research anonymously among public sources, thereby completely avoiding a potential accusation of improper data acquisition.

## How to Use the Net for Competitive Intelligence

The standard CI research method (as set forth, for example, in Leonard Fuld's book *Competitor Intelligence*, http://www.fuld.com) starts with gathering information from basic sources and expands toward using creative

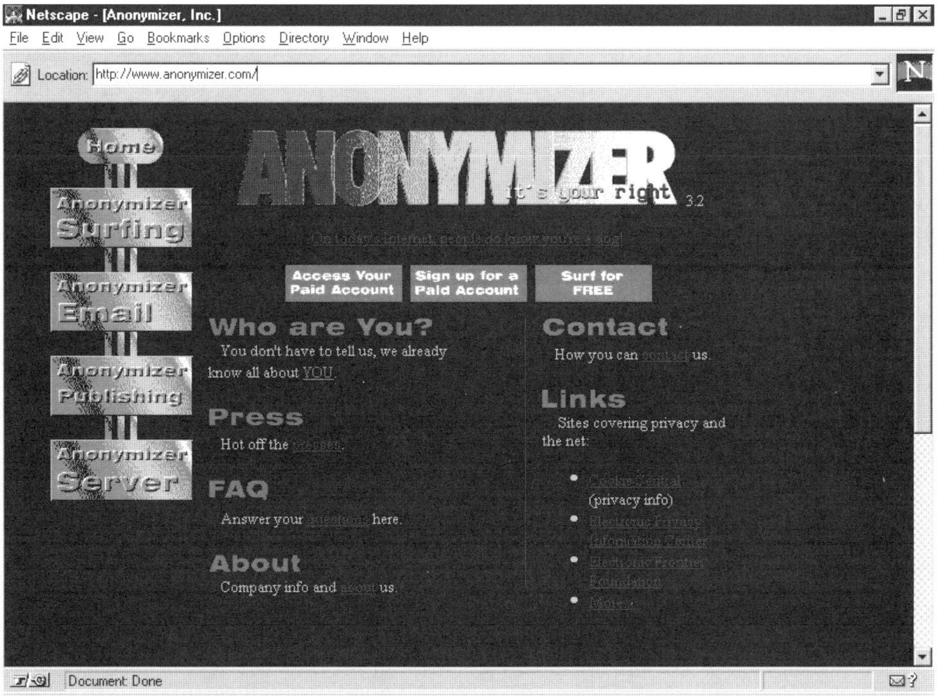




**FIGURE 10.1.** The Anonymizer site enables you to surf the Net as if you are using its computer instead of yours. In this way, the sites you visit are unable to record your true identity.

sources. The Internet fits into both phases of this process. As you gain experience in using the Net for research, you will learn to determine when the Net is an appropriate source for particular kinds of data, and when you ought to use non-Internet sources.

Basic sources for CI include the traditional materials researchers look to. Such sources include materials from competitors themselves, governmental filings and industrial reports, periodicals and directories, financial industry data, association materials, and various databases. Creative sources include telephone directories (including reverse and crisscross directories), visual observations, trade shows, UCC filings, and classified ads.

Thinking like a researcher in the context of CI involves thinking about who would monitor or care about the target subject. Who would want to catalog such information? Where would they catalog it? Combine this thought process with the basic and creative sources available on the Internet and elsewhere.

### Basic Sources

The first step in using the Net for CI is to conduct a broad search to find the most obvious sources. Start with keyword searches in various indexes (AltaVista, Infoseek, WebCrawler, and so on) to see what turns up. Among the most common and easiest-to-use sources you will find by searching the indexes are competitor Web sites. Beyond company sites, the Internet provides a range of company information sources. (Refer to Chapter 9 in this book.) Another fine starting point is the Internet Intelligence Index provided by Fuld & Company (http://www.fuld.com). Fuld provides a collection of links to a very broad range of basic business resources.

Current news is a natural place to find out what competitors are up to. Many companies put news releases on their home page. For more objective insights, try Ecola's Newsstand (http://www.ecola.com/news), which links to some four thousand paper periodical Web sites. CNN Interactive (http://www.cnn.com) is another good source of current news. (Refer also to Chapter 6 in this book.)

Regulatory agencies at all levels collect information on companies. Often, vital product and plant intelligence as well as records of complaints and investigations will be found in these Internet data warehouses. An excellent starting point for government filings is the Federal Web Locator (http://www.law.vill.edu/fed-agency/fedwebloc.html) provided by Villanova University, which seeks to link to every U.S. government agency. Among the most useful federal government sites is the SEC's EDGAR system (http://www.sec.gov/edgarhp.htm), which provides the public company filings required by securities legislation. Such filings can provide significant insight into company operations. In addition, since these filings are required by law, they have a certain amount of assumed accuracy. Some company reports available commercially, including some Dun & Bradstreet (D&B) reports, for example, contain self-reported data that is not required by law, but rather is elicited by (in this case) D&B. It is fair to say that a good researcher is a skeptical researcher. Whenever possible, get independent verification for all information you need to depend on.

Another potentially useful government agency, the Occupational Safety and Health Administration (OSHA) at http://www.osha.gov/, provides, among many other valuable free resources, Hazard Information Bulletins by month for the past twelve years. (See Figure 10.2.) These bulletins identify manufacturers whose products have caused injury and death. If you are aiming to identify a competitor's weak points, these OSHA bulletins can make a sharp impression.

The U.S. Department of Commerce (DOC) at http://www.doc.gov/ provides reams and reams of information via the Net. The number of bureaus

**FIGURE 10.2.** OSHA provides bulletins identifying products that have caused injury and death. These bulletins are accessible on the Net.

and agencies that fall within the DOC's jurisdiction is staggering. There are testimony and export schedules and regulations and on and on. Knowing how to get around amid government data is a specialty unto itself.

Regional Chamber of Commerce offices may also have data concerning particular companies. There are several Web pages that collect such links (for example, http://www.chamber-of-commerce.com/).

Industry watchdogs and agencies may be monitoring your target company. You might want to search through the online collections of unions and associations (http://www.aflcio.org/ or http://www.asaenet.org/gateway/onlineassocslist.html). Yahoo also maintains an extensive professional association list (http://www.yahoo.com/Business_and_Economy/Organizations/Professional/).

Finding information by industry is often best started using an existing index. Again, Fuld (http://www.fuld.com) provides a good starting point for industry data in its Internet Intelligence Index. Another good approach for researching industry developments is to find companies and universities that conduct research in that field. For example, if you need to find out about chemical industry developments, use a search engine or directory to find your way to chemical companies, research organizations, and academic departments that make information available online.

### Creative Sources

Since the Internet is a new medium, it lends itself very well to creative research. Virtually every sector of society—including government, nonprofits, public and private companies, and religious and secular organizations—is looking for ways to take advantage of the Internet's multimedia, interactive, and international features. As a result, a lot of different sorts of information are provided on the Net, and you can turn this to your research advantage.

For example, the many classified and job advertisement sites on the Net are excellent places to scope out competitors. You may find that a competitor is trying to fill new positions in a brand-new business area. Alternatively, a rival might be trying to fill key positions that have recently been vacated (although no public announcement was made).

Say you represent a telecommunications company that competes with MCI. In the course of your representation, you want to know what sort of new initiatives MCI is undertaking. While scouring the MCI site for clues, you discover the Employment Opportunities page (http://www.mci.com/aboutmci/career/), which MCI uses to recruit new employees. You notice that the job openings are searchable by job category and by state. It so happens that your client is particularly concerned about a suspected new research and development facility being built by MCI in northern California. In your research you discover that, in fact, MCI has posted numerous ads for exotically skilled engineers in Sacramento, thereby lending credence to your client's concerns. You also notice that MCI is hiring commercial law attorneys, and you weigh the possibilities.

Another creative intelligence-gathering technique is the use of e-mail. E-mail is an easy way to communicate with experts, reporters, analysts, insiders, educators, and players in specific industries and markets. You can use e-mail to solicit opinions, explanations, comments, and even rumors. You might use e-mail to contact journalists writing company profiles or researching new markets.

One of the completely unique-to-the-Net techniques you can try is to find out what Web sites link to your competitor's page. This technique may alert you to previously unknown strategic alliances or may open up a market for your client's products that had not been foreseen. Use Digital's AltaVista search engine for its Advanced Search feature, which indicates the pages that link to a particular URL. For example, go to http://altavista.digital.com and type in the search box link:http://www.whitecase.com/. You will be able to see how many pages point to White & Case's home page. This may indicate alliances and may otherwise provide you with insight about the firm.

### Discussion Forums

Another way to leverage the Internet's uniqueness is to take advantage of the many newsgroups and mailing lists. For example, you might post a message in one of these discussion forums, asking a question about your client's competitor. Then, sit back and monitor the responses. You might consider using forums that are very narrow in their scope, like banking in Britain (uk.finance), or you could try broader discussion areas, such as alt.business, alt.business.importexport, or biz.marketplace.international.

Conduct keyword searches of the newsgroup search engines (http://www.dejanews.com/, http://altavista.digital.com/, and http://www.infoseek.com/) to determine what is being said about your target. The target company may even be posting messages. It is not unusual for companies to conduct informal opinion polls to test interest in a developing concept.

# CHAPTER ELEVEN

# How to Conduct Medical Research on the Net

## Why Medical Research?

Successful personal injury and medical malpractice actions usually require lawyers to consult with health care professionals. The opinions of experts who have direct clinical experience, for example, can provide invaluable perspective on the complex world of medicine. However, complete dependence on experts can risk the lawyer's ability to retain control of the case. If you are not aware, for example, that the medical procedure being discussed has been performed for several decades, you might not know to question your own expert's statement that the procedure is "relatively new." Therefore, to complement medical expert opinions, an awareness of the specific medical issues in question is essential.

Rapid change in the complex health care industry is another source of work for lawyers. In response to the costs of health care, new types of organizations, jobs, equipment, and procedures are changing the profession on a regular basis. Such disturbances to the status quo can result in legal disputes, for example, pitting the quality of care against health care company interests in profit making. Recent issues include the responsibilities of managed care companies; the displacement of traditional jobs (like nurses) by new, often less-experienced workers; and pharmaceutical company liability. As the industry evolves, so will the nature of disputes and contracts handled by lawyers who practice in the health-related fields. Lawyers will need to understand the new issues and arguments relative to hospital and physician liability and standard treatment guidelines for common conditions. The Internet is an excellent reference source to enhance such understanding.

The medical research materials available free on the Internet are both broad and deep. Such materials cover a very broad array of health care subjects, and often the materials go way beyond the superficial, providing significant depth and insight into medical issues. Available resources include the entire physician database from the American Medical Association, listing over 650,000 U.S. physicians; glossaries to help you navigate through medical jargon; and detailed anatomical and procedural collections that can provide what you need to understand the facts of medically related legal matters.

## GLOSSARIES

Health care professionals, like lawyers, have a language all their own. Some of the most respected and comprehensive medical references, such as *Dorland's Illustrated Medical Dictionary,* are not yet free on the Net, although there are several glossaries that are easily accessible at any time. Some of the glossaries are specific to areas of medicine, and some are general. The following list offers a few of the available terminology references:

### General Medical Glossaries

Dr. Schueler's Searchable Online Medical Glossary—This glossary is very easy to use and provides consumer-level definitions of a comprehensive collection of terms.

http://www.drschueler.com/glossary/glossary.htm

Information Network, Inc.—A very simple glossary.

http://www.medicinenet.com/mainmenu/Glossary/Gloss_A.htm

Martindale's Health Science Guide—This guide offers a list of various other medical dictionaries.

http://www-sci.lib.uci.edu/HSG/Medical.html#DICTION

### Specialized Glossaries

HMO Glossary—Cutting through managed care industry jargon is important when prosecuting or defending a health maintenance organization (HMO), for example. It is common to come across four-syllable words for simple concepts, and it seems that each new type of provider creates a three-letter acronym: PPO, PSO, IPA, and so forth. The HMO Glossary defines words and acronyms that have unique meanings in the managed care context.

http://www.bcm.tmc.edu/ama-mss/glossary.html

Foreign Language Medical Glossary—For medical terms in foreign languages, this online dictionary (in nine European languages) is available.

http://allserv.rug.ac.be/~rvdstich/eugloss/EN/lijst.html

## MEDICAL TEXTS

To quickly get up to speed in unfamiliar medical territory, a medical textbook can be ideal. Texts will generally provide broad as well as detailed descriptions of diseases and procedures. The date of publication of the text will identify the point after which more recent journal articles are useful. Just as pocket parts are essential to knowing the current state of the law, so recent medical developments are found in the journals.

There are many collections of medical information on the Net. They are organized by body part, disease, or area of medicine, and they function quite well as introductions and as general starting points for medical research on the Net.

### General

Martindale's Health Science Guide—This is one of the most comprehensive sites among the many medical indexes; there is even a dental and veterinary index. The amount of information accessible through these pages is staggering, but, organizationally, the site leaves a bit to be desired. It lacks a search engine, so you need to scroll and click through a number of pages to reach your destination. Despite this flaw, Martindale's provides a wealth of free information.

http://www-sci.lib.uci.edu/HSG/Medical.html

The Multimedia Medical Reference Library—Here is another broad medical index. This site is searchable, very extensive, and, in general, a good place to start out learning about particular aspects of medicine.

http://www.med-library.com/

### Anatomy

The Digital Anatomist—The Department of Biological Structure at the University of Washington provides two- and three-dimensional views of various organs reconstructed from cadaver sections, MRI scans, and computer reconstructions.

http://www9.biostr.washington.edu/da.html

Human Anatomy Online—As you move your cursor over the body, a Java applet displays the name of the body part. When you click on the name, a clear description is displayed. When you click on the tiny looking glass icon within the name window, you get a closeup lateral view of the body part.

http://www.innerbody.com/

Martindale's Health Science Guide—Martindale's anatomy page offers an extensive collection of anatomy atlases from medical schools and other organizations throughout the world. Here you will find body parts, interactive anatomy browsers, anatomy animation and images, and anatomy tutorials by body parts and systems.

http://www-sci.lib.uci.edu/HSG/MedicalAnatomy.html#AIB

The Visible Human Project—The National Library of Medicine's plan to create complete, anatomically detailed, three-dimensional representations of the male and female human body has resulted in this fascinating source. (See Figure 11.1.) The images available from the project are all cross-sectional and may not be as useful as isolated, three-dimensional images.

http://www.nlm.nih.gov/research/visible/visible_human.htm

### Diseases and Procedures

The Merck Manual of Diagnosis and Therapies—The Merck Manual is a primary source of information on any disease. It describes symptoms, common clinical procedures, laboratory tests, and virtually all the disorders that a general internist might encounter. Current therapy is pre-

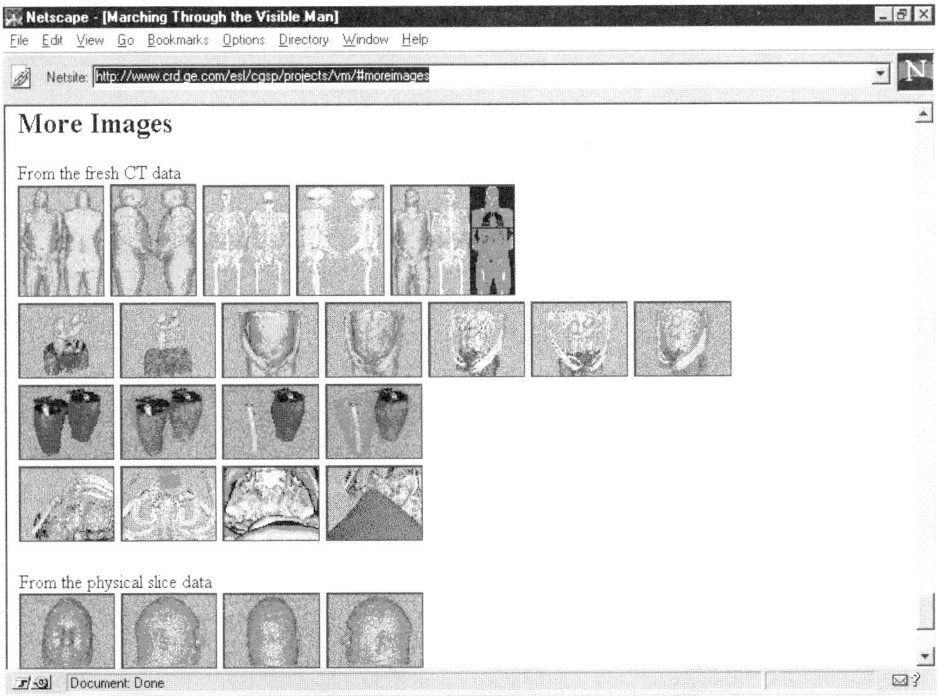


**FIGURE 11.1.** The Visible Human Project presents a unique, free opportunity to become familiar with human anatomy.

sented for each disorder and supplemented with a separate section on clinical pharmacology. Merck provides the manual on the Internet in searchable, full-text form without charge. (See Figure 11.2.)

http://www.merck.com/!!rJfJw0ayFrJfJw0ayF/pubs/mmanual/html/sectoc.htm

Centers for Disease Control—The CDC provides a searchable site that is useful for clinical descriptions of and treatments for diseases.

http://www.cdc.gov/diseases/diseases.html

Martindale's Health Science Guide—This source organizes diseases and conditions by medical specialty. The site concentrates on proper diagnosis and treatment.

http://www-sci.lib.uci.edu/HSG/Medical.html

Oncolink—The University of Pennsylvania Cancer Center presents this site, providing general and specific cancer information. The site is not extensive, but if it addresses your subject, it generally does so well. Informa-

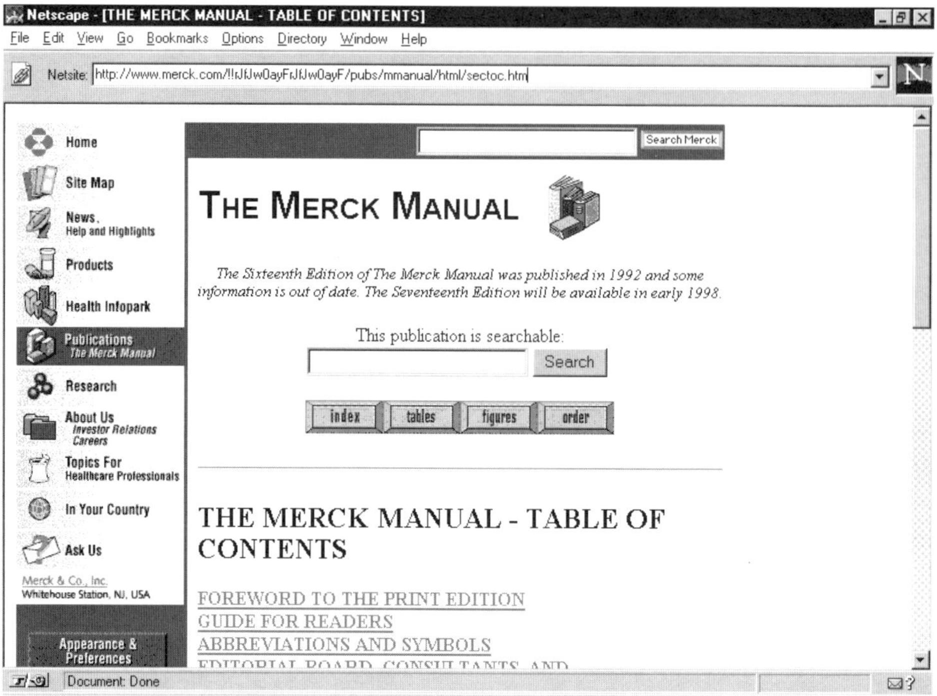




**FIGURE 11.2.** The Merck Manual describes virtually all the disorders that a general internist might encounter. This is an excellent, free Internet resource.

tion is provided on pediatric and adult cancers, descriptions and stage explanations of disease, and treatment options. In addition, a "Clinical Trials" page discusses new treatments under evaluation.

http://cancer.med.upenn.edu/

Virtual Hospital—This is a service of the University of Iowa Medical School's Radiology Department. The portion of the site designated "For Healthcare Providers" is a multimedia textbook, offering clinical procedural guidelines arranged by organ system.

http://www.vh.org/

## JOURNAL AND ARTICLE RESOURCES

Once you have consulted a medical text and developed a basic understanding of your subject, you may wish to review more-current materials. Or, you may have only a limited amount of time and require an overview article on a particular medical subject. Journal articles are an excellent way to learn about current medical thinking. The "card catalog" of medical journal articles is known as Medline. It is one of the primary sources of information on the world's biomedical literature, containing article references from more than thirty-five hundred biomedical journals. Medline is a bibliographical index, and, as such, it does not include the full text of each article. However, about 75 percent of the references include summaries of the articles. The database draws on international sources, and so some Medline-referenced articles are not in English. Medline is available on NEXIS and DIALOG for a fee, and it is searchable free on the Net (http://www.nlm.nih.gov/).

Since Medline does not provide actual journal articles but rather abstracts and the citation required to retrieve articles from medical libraries, researchers may wish to go directly to the Web sites of particular journals. Some journals do not provide full-text articles, others provide full-text articles of the current issue only, and others provide current articles as well as archives. Each journal has a different agenda for its Web site. Some seek to invite contributions, some want subscribers, some are willing to give material away free online. The following is a list of prominent medical journal Web sites:

Clinical Nutrition Articles

http://netspace.net.au/~helmant/nut_art1.htm

Journal of the American Medical Association

http://www.ama-assn.org/public/journals/jama/jamahome.htm

Index of International Medical Journals

http://www.priory.com/journals/

New England Journal of Medicine On-line

http://www.nejm.org/

Medical Reporter—Patient oriented.

http://www.dash.com/netro/nwx/tmr/tmr.html

MedWeb: Electronic Newsletters and Journals

http://www.cc.emory.edu/WHSCL/medweb.ejs.html

## NEW MEDICAL DEVELOPMENT RESOURCES

Medical Breakthroughs—If you are researching a rapidly evolving area of medicine, this site may be useful. It offers the latest-breaking medical news. E-mail updates on the latest breakthroughs are also available here.

http://www.ivanhoe.com

Drugs in Development—The Pharmaceutical Research and Manufacturers Association provides this searchable (by disease, indication, or drug) database.

http://www.phrma.org/webdb/help.htm

Reuters Health Information Services—This is a great source of medical news of the moment. News is focused for health professionals and consumers.

http://www.reutershealth.com/

## MEDICAL DEVICE RESOURCES

Health Industry Manufacturers Association

http://www.himanet.com/

Medical Device Link

http://www.devicelink.com/

## PHARMACEUTICAL RESOURCES

Clinical Pharmacology Online

http://www.cponline.gsm.com/

Drug Database—This index of generic and named pharmaceuticals is not comprehensive, but handy. Listings include indications and manufacturers.

http://pharminfo.com/drugdb/

Drug Interaction Search

http://www.rxlist.com/interact.htm

Internet Drug Index

http://www.rxlist.com/

MedicineNet—Information provided includes side effects, precautions, proper use, prescribed purposes, and drug class.

http://www.medicinenet.com/MAINMENU/pharmacy/pharm_a.htm

## HEALTH PROFESSION RESOURCES

### Physician Directories

American Medical Association—The AMA provides the primary physician directory available to the public. For information on individual doctors, choose Physician Select. All 650,000 accredited doctors in the United States are represented. Information provided includes address, phone number, specialty, where degrees were obtained, and where residencies were served. (See Figure 11.3.)

http://www.ama-assn.org/

Physician Identifier Number Database—Federal law provides for the unique numbering of physicians who provide services for which payment

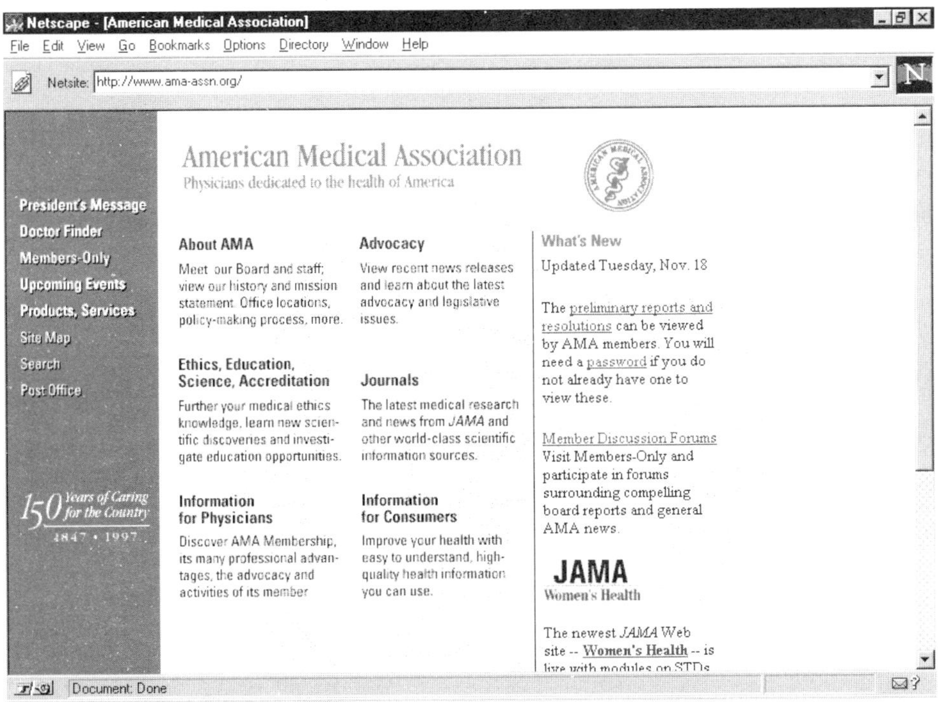


**FIGURE 11.3.** Use AMA Physician Select to locate a doctor by name, specialty, and location from the 650,000 physicians licensed to practice in the United States.

is made under Medicare. The publication of a directory of the numbers is also required by law. The directory does not include residents, interns, or physicians practicing solely within a health maintenance organization, but it does contain information on physicians in both solo and group practice. The directory provided on the Internet by the Medical College of Wisconsin can be searched by state and keyword (typically the physician's last name). For each physician, the database provides medical specialty, state and zip code, and identification number.

http://www.cpg.mcw.edu/www/upin.html

Physician Locator—For those physicians who have elected to provide data, this source may provide more info per physician than the AMA database.

http://www.medaccess.com/physician/phys01.htm

### Physician Licensing and Disciplinary Actions

New York Professional Licenses—The New York State Department of Education provides access to New York State licensing and disciplinary action data for health care professionals, including physicians, dentists, chiropractors, nurses, optometrists, and more.

http://www.nysed.gov/prof/profhome.htm

New York Disciplinary Actions—The State Health Department issues these monthly reports listing doctors who have been subject to disciplinary actions in New York State. There is also a searchable index of disciplined physicians here.

http://www.health.state.ny.us/nysdoh/opmc/main.htm

### Other Health Professions

American Chiropractic Association

http://www.cais.net/aca/

American Dental Association

http://www.ada.org/

American Nurses Association

http://www.ana.org/

American Optometric Association

http://www.aoanet.org/aoanet/

American Physical Therapy Association

http://www.apta.org/

Nurse Practitioners

http://www.unh.edu/npract/index.html

### ■ SUCCESS STORY: KEVIN GRIERSON

Attorney Kevin Grierson of Jones, Blechman, Woltz & Kelly of Newport News, Virginia, has used the AMA site with success. In particular, he has "had some luck locating information on debtors. We had a doctor in a medical malpractice case pick up and move on us, and I was able to find his current job through the AMA's physician directory, even though he wasn't a member of the AMA." ■

## MEDICAL METASITES

Food and Drug Administration—The FDA provides regulatory guidance, lists of approved drugs, news concerning new medical procedures, and more.

http://www.fda.gov/

Jeff Flax's Medical Resources

http://shell.rmi.net/~jflax/jmf_med.htm

Yahoo Medical Sites

http://www.yahoo.com/Health/Medicine/

# CHAPTER TWELVE

## Moving Ahead

FROM OUR VANTAGE POINT in the late twentieth century, a few things seem clear. The Internet will become so ubiquitous and comprehensive that it will become the sole e-mail and electronic information source. It will become our primary link to world media, to literature, and to news. We will use it to conduct business and to keep in touch with friends and family from anywhere at any time.

Driving this pervasive usage will be access. While use of the Net is now limited to those with enough affluence, education, and patience to acquire and use computers, the Internet will someday become as accessible as the telephone, at airports, coffee shops, and street corner kiosks. It will be available via inexpensive devices already in our homes, including the telephone and television.

All electronic information sources will be available through the Internet. It will be unnecessary to have relationships with several database vendors to access their data. Through the single Internet portal, access will be provided to all publications and databases. If we wish to purchase something from a publisher, we will do so on a single-transaction basis, using an electronic money account, just as we use credit cards today to purchase catalog items over the telephone. There will be no need for special database access software developed by and shipped from each publisher. The software we use to access the Net will become as simple and transparent as the television gadgetry that sends pictures, sound, and text into our lives.

Security, encryption, and authentication will advance to the point where it is push-button-simple to use. We will know to a high degree of certainty that our data transmissions are bulletproof. There will be a marked reduction in the number of people who hand-notarize documents, who maintain warehouses of paper documents, and who physically carry documents from place to place. No doubt, these functions will be replaced by people and machines that perform similar functions using electronic rather than physical means. Notarization, for example, will occur with an electronic stamp, certifying the authorship, electronic signature, or authenticity of electronic documents.

The concerns surrounding data theft and interception will be replaced by a higher level of confidence than we now have in certified, traceable postal mail. While there will always be some exploitable hole in the data transmission network, eventually we will be able to send documents via e-mail and receive an instantaneous confirmation that the message is safely waiting for the intended recipient. And unlike some physical documents that are absolutely unique, electronic documents that get swept away by a human, mechanical, or natural act can be retrieved, unencrypted, and precisely duplicated from the backup technology that will record our electronic activities.

This latter development gives rise to a raft of new concerns. For example, the inability to know that a particular document has been destroyed can discourage the documentation of ideas. Even if ideas are not proposed seriously, if they are preserved, they may haunt us. As Bob Dylan once put it: "If my thought-dreams could be seen, they'd probably put my head in a guillotine." For example, if a corporate executive uses his or her computer to draft corporate plans, the computer file may be viewed, in some later litigation, as evidence of corporate intent or knowledge. If backup technology saves those plans in perpetuity, they could be discoverable and injurious to corporate interests.

Privacy is another concern raised by electronic tracking. The more activities we conduct using computers, whether they record our credit card transactions, our e-mail correspondence, or our electronic toll payments on the highway, the more our activities are recorded and reviewable. A balance must be struck between the interests of society, corporations, and law enforcement and the right of the individual, as Justice Brandeis put it, "to be let alone."

The Internet will have a revolutionary impact on lawyers' ability to access information. The Internet's cheap and accessible publishing platform allows anyone to distribute material around the globe. Whether the material includes court opinions, deposition transcripts, or government filings, so long as it is not private, anyone can publish it on the Net. The large, highly capitalized publishers who have historically sold access to noncopyrightable public data will become vulnerable to upstart companies and governments who accumulate, categorize, and provide free access to the databases lawyers need. The sort of factual information described in this book will continue to be freely available via the Internet. Or, where information is not free, its cost will be reduced to the micro-transactional level. We will pay pennies for information that has some added value, based on the credibility of the source, the goodwill of a brand name, or features added by the publisher.

Information will become a commodity. Consumers will be able to access the same laws and facts that lawyers do. The opportunity, then, will be in interpreting the law in the factual context to best advantage. D.C. attorney Cleveland Thornton says it well:

> A lot of what lawyers do is, in a strange kind of way, a middle management function. We are the gatekeepers to information, and we also play a role in giving advice. I think the gatekeeper part is going to be a lot less important. The advice part, interpreting information and being that type of source, will still be valuable. When you start using computers and you really do it right so you can start writing wills and contracts [using] expert applications, that type of thing is probably not going to involve lawyers as much as in the past because the simple fact is that you can write programs that a layperson could use as well as most lawyers, and also make it so that you can do things like contacting the courthouse from your own computer to see who filed information and also to do title searches—who owns what piece of land—without having to go through either a lawyer or a title search company. I think that is going to give people more control over their lives and less of a need for lawyers.
>
> I think [the Internet] makes it easier to do research. I do not think it makes it easier to do legal research. If I had a brief to write, I would have to use WESTLAW or LEXIS. Once you get rid of West's [page number copyright] monopoly, then it is not going to be very difficult to have the cases on the Internet. You can already do [Internet] searches on statutes as well as you can on LEXIS or WESTLAW. You do have to know what you are doing. What is easier, I think, is looking up other things that are peripheral to the particular, hard-core legal search. That is a lot easier.
>
> [For example,] I saw a movie the other night about Isadora Duncan. I had heard of her but I did not know much about her, and after the movie I did a quick search on the Internet. I found a couple of really good biographies. They were put out by some schools of dance and various universities. I found out some things that I did not know—questions that I had during the movie. It had nothing to do with a client. But that kind of peripheral research might affect your practice.

Finally, the most exciting things about the Internet are the new opportunities it presents. While we need to recognize the responsibilities created by such opportunities, the potential enhancements to our lives fire the imagination. For example, the ability of software agents to anticipate our interests, to filter through the information ocean to find just what we need to know, is a genuine time-saver. Imagine getting real-time stock prices on shares you own, or news about your client's takeover candidate while you are taking care of daily business.

There are already some three dozen companies providing such personalized information via e-mail and news ticker. My.yahoo.com (see Figure 12.1) and the free clipping service provided by Excite (go to **http://www.excite.com**, click on the News icon, and then click on "Free Clipping Service") are two examples.

The online community is another Internet innovation that truly makes use of technology in a new way. Online technology enables people from disparate geographic communities to instantly and easily communicate with each other. Electronic mailing lists and newsgroups represent a

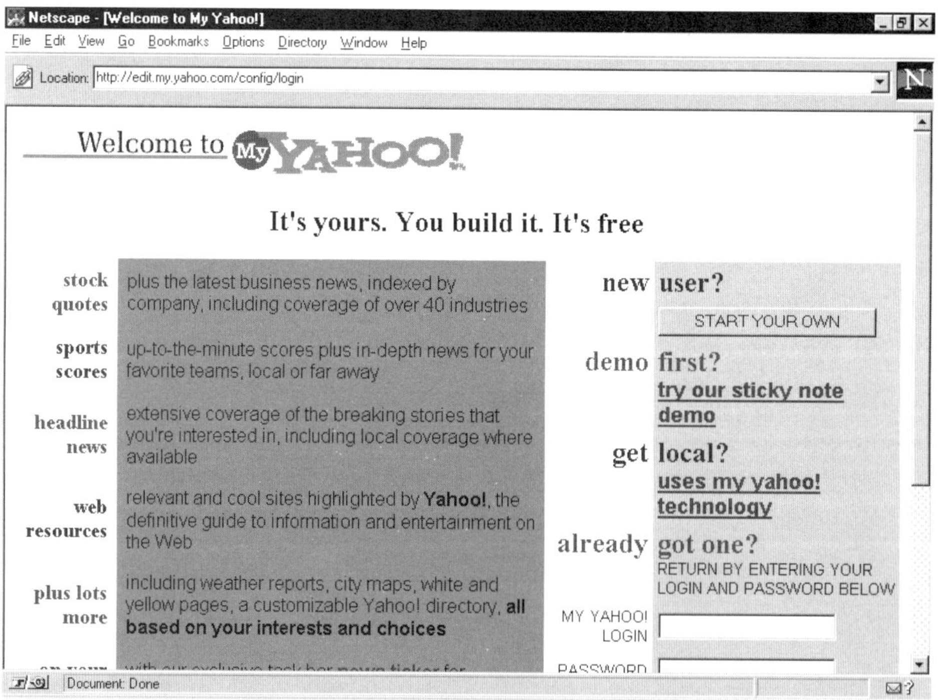




**FIGURE 12.1.** My Yahoo is a free, personalized information service that sends alerts concerning subject matter you ask for, including news, stock quotes, and sports scores.

truly interactive phenomenon, where people use technology to do useful things (talk to each other and share ideas, for example) that they could not do as easily before. Future innovations will find additional, remarkable ways for people to use Internet technology to work with each other.

This is surely an exciting time. We are in the midst of dramatic change brought about by new technology. The lives of lawyers and those we work with will never be the same.

# Index

# *Order Form*

| Qty | Title | LPM Price | Regular Price | Total |
|---|---|---|---|---|
| ______ | ABA Guide to Lawyer Trust Accounts (5110374) | $ 69.95 | $ 79.95 | $________ |
| ______ | ABA Guide to Prof. Managers in the Law Office (5110373) | 69.95 | 79.95 | $________ |
| ______ | Billing Innovations (5110366) | 124.95 | 144.95 | $________ |
| ______ | Changing Jobs, 2nd Ed. (5110334) | 49.95 | 59.95 | $________ |
| ______ | Compensation Plans for Lawyers, 2nd Ed. (5110353) | 69.95 | 79.95 | $________ |
| ______ | Computer-Assisted Legal Research (5110388) | 69.95 | 79.95 | $________ |
| ______ | Connecting with Your Client (5110378) | 54.95 | 64.95 | $________ |
| ______ | Do-It-Yourself Public Relations (5110352) | 69.95 | 79.95 | $________ |
| ______ | Finding the Right Lawyer (5110339) | 19.95 | 19.95 | $________ |
| ______ | Flying Solo, 2nd Ed. (5110328) | 59.95 | 69.95 | $________ |
| ______ | How to Draft Bills Clients Rush to Pay (5110344) | 39.95 | 49.95 | $________ |
| ______ | How to Start & Build a Law Practice, 3rd Ed. (5110293) | 32.95 | 39.95 | $________ |
| ______ | Law Office Policy & Procedures Manual (5110375) | 99.95 | 109.95 | $________ |
| ______ | Lawyer's Guide to Creating Web Pages (5110383) | 54.95 | 64.95 | $________ |
| ______ | Lawyer's Guide to the Internet (5110343) | 24.95 | 29.95 | $________ |
| ______ | Lawyer's Guide to Marketing on the Internet (5110371) | 54.95 | 64.95 | $________ |
| ______ | Lawyer's Quick Guide to Microsoft Internet® Explorer (5110392) | 24.95 | 29.95 | $________ |
| ______ | Lawyer's Quick Guide to Netscape® Navigator (5110384) | 24.95 | 29.95 | $________ |
| ______ | Lawyer's Quick Guide to WordPerfect® 7.0/8.0 (5110395) | 34.95 | 39.95 | $________ |
| ______ | Leaders' Digest (5110356) | 49.95 | 59.95 | $________ |
| ______ | Living with the Law (5110379) | 59.95 | 69.95 | $________ |
| ______ | Practicing Law Without Clients (5110376) | 49.95 | 59.95 | $________ |
| ______ | Running a Law Practice on a Shoestring (5110387) | 39.95 | 49.95 | $________ |
| ______ | Survival Guide for Road Warriors (5110362) | 24.95 | 29.95 | $________ |
| ______ | Through the Client's Eyes (5110337) | 69.95 | 79.95 | $________ |
| ______ | Women Rainmakers' 101+ Best Marketing Tips (5110336) | 14.95 | 19.95 | $________ |

| *HANDLING | | **TAX | | |
|---|---|---|---|---|
| $10.00-$24.99 . . . $3.95 | | DC residents add 5.75% | SUBTOTAL: | $________ |
| $25.00-$49.99 . . . $4.95 | | IL residents add 8.75% | *HANDLING: | $________ |
| $50.00+ . . . . . . . . $5.95 | | MD residents add 5% | **TAX: | $________ |
| | | | TOTAL: | $________ |

**PAYMENT**

☐ Check enclosed (to the ABA) ☐ Bill Me

☐ Visa ☐ MasterCard ☐ American Express Account Number:______________________________

Exp. Date:____________ Signature______________________________

Name______________________________

Firm______________________________

Address______________________________

City______________________________ State____________________ ZIP__________

Phone number______________________________

**Mail to:** ABA Publication Orders
P.O. Box 10892
Chicago, IL 60610-0892

**Phone:** (800) 285-2221 **Fax:** (312) 988-5568

**World Wide Web:** http//www.abanet.org/lpm/catalog
**Email:** abasvcctr@abanet.org

THE SECTION OF LAW PRACTICE MANAGEMENT

# CUSTOMER COMMENT FORM

ABA

Title of Book: ______________________________

We've tried to make this publication as useful, accurate, and readable as possible. Please take 5 minutes to tell us if we succeeded. Your comments and suggestions will help us improve our publications. Thank you!

1. How did you acquire this publication:

| | | |
|---|---|---|
| ☐ by mail order | ☐ at a meeting/convention | ☐ as a gift |
| ☐ by phone order | ☐ at a bookstore | ☐ don't know |

☐ other: (describe) ______________________________

Please rate this publication as follows:

| | Excellent | Good | Fair | Poor | Not Applicable |
|---|---|---|---|---|---|
| **Readability**: Was the book easy to read and understand? | ☐ | ☐ | ☐ | ☐ | ☐ |
| **Examples/Cases**: Were they helpful, practical? Were there enough? | ☐ | ☐ | ☐ | ☐ | ☐ |
| **Content**: Did the book meet your expectations? Did it cover the subject adequately? | ☐ | ☐ | ☐ | ☐ | ☐ |
| **Organization and clarity**: Was the sequence of text logical? Was it easy to find what you wanted to know? | ☐ | ☐ | ☐ | ☐ | ☐ |
| **Illustrations/forms/checklists**: Were they clear and useful? Were there enough? | ☐ | ☐ | ☐ | ☐ | ☐ |
| **Physical attractiveness**: What did you think of the appearance of the publication (typesetting, printing, etc.)? | ☐ | ☐ | ☐ | ☐ | ☐ |

Would you recommend this book to another attorney/administrator? ☐ Yes ☐ No

How could this publication be improved? What else would you like to see in it?

______________________________

______________________________

______________________________

Do you have other comments or suggestions? ______________________________

______________________________

______________________________

Name ______________________________

Firm/Company ______________________________

Address ______________________________

City/State/Zip ______________________________

Phone ______________________________

Firm Size: ______________ Area of specialization: ______________________________

**We appreciate your time and help.**

Fold

NO POSTAGE
NECESSARY
IF MAILED
IN THE
UNITED STATES

**BUSINESS REPLY MAIL**

FIRST CLASS PERMIT NO. 16471 CHICAGO, ILLINOIS

*POSTAGE WILL BE PAID BY ADDRESSEE*

AMERICAN BAR ASSOCIATION
PPM, 8TH FLOOR
750 N. LAKE SHORE DRIVE
CHICAGO, ILLINOIS 60611-9851

Fold